MY FATHER
LEFT ME
IRELAND

MY FATHER LEFT ME IRELAND

An American Son's Search for Home

MICHAEL BRENDAN DOUGHERTY

SENTINEL

Sentinel
An imprint of Penguin Random House LLC
penguinrandomhouse.com

Most Sentinel books are available at a discount when purchased in quantity
for sales promotions or corporate use. Special editions, which include
personalized covers, excerpts, and corporate imprints, can be created when
purchased in large quantities. For more information, please call (212) 572-2232
or email specialmarkets@penguinrandomhouse.com. Your local bookstore can
also assist with discounted bulk purchases using the Penguin Random House
corporate Business-to-Business program. For assistance in locating a
participating retailer, email B2B@penguinrandomhouse.com.

LIBRARY OF CONGRESS CATALOGING-IN-PUBLICATION DATA
Names: Dougherty, Michael Brendan, author.
Title: My father left me Ireland: an American son's search for home /
Michael Brendan Dougherty.
Description: New York, New York: Sentinel, an imprint of
Penguin Random House LLC, [2019]
Identifiers: LCCN 2018060865 | ISBN 9780525538653 (hardcover)
Subjects: LCSH: Dougherty, Michael Brendan. | Irish Americans--Biography. |
Irish Americans--Ethnic identity. | Children of single parents--United States--
Biography. | Father and child. | Irish Americans--Social life and customs. |
Irish language--Study and teaching--Anecdotes. | Acculturation. |
Nationalism--Ireland. | Ireland--Civilization.
Classification: LCC E184.I6 D635 2019 | DDC 305.8916/2073--dc23
LC record available at https://lccn.loc.gov/2018060865

Printed in the United States of America
1 3 5 7 9 10 8 6 4 2

BOOK DESIGN BY LUCIA BERNARD

Penguin is committed to publishing works of quality and integrity.
In that spirit, we are proud to offer this book to our readers; however,
the story, the experiences, and the words are the author's alone.

For my mother, Maryellen

Contents

A man who is a mere author is nothing. If there is anything good in anything I have written, it is the potentiality of adventure in me.

—Thomas MacDonagh

INTRODUCTION

I've been told all my life that I didn't need my father. He had left my American mother to bring me up by herself in New Jersey while he raised a family of his own back in Ireland. I was encouraged to believe that I was better off without him, that my broken home was just another modern family, no worse than any other.

But when my wife became pregnant with our first child, I suddenly realized that I was a vital link between my unborn daughter and her heritage. And I realized that my own father was that link for me, whether I liked it or not.

In my father's absence, my mother tried to give me some sense of my Irishness. She would sing about the heroic sacrifices made for Irish freedom. She gave me the sense that out there, beyond our broken home, there was a homeland, a heritage, a patrimony.

At one point in my life, I had believed what the world told me—that the idea of a homeland saved at a great price was just a harmful myth. A prominent Irish leader reiterated that view not so long ago: "Sacrifice breeds intransigence," he said, "The dead exert an unhealthy power over the living, persuading the living to hold out for the impossible, so that the sacrifice of the dead is not perceived to have been in vain."

But when I heard those words a few months before my daughter was born, I knew in my bones that he was wrong.

I don't think I'm alone. We live in an age of disinheritance, with longings that we're discouraged from acknowledging. This book of letters is my attempt at rekindling a relationship between father and son, at recovering something in danger of being lost. I wrote these to help my children have a proper home, and to know the refuge and comfort of a homeland beyond it.

I

Only Child, Single Mother

Come away, O human child!
To the waters and the wild with a faery, hand in hand,
For the world's more full of weeping than you can understand.

—*W. B. Yeats, "The Stolen Child"*

Dear Father,

Do you remember when you put the hurl into my hand? I was six, I think. It was a gray day in Clare, a kind of gray I never saw at home in America. I remember the shabby carpet of the shop's floor and a mumbled instruction to put my hands at my side. A number of these hurls—these wooden axes used in a sport I did not know— were held up to my body for sizing. I couldn't understand much of what the men in the shop were saying. Their thick Irish accents, so different from yours, meant that in the whole world as I perceived it, I only understood you and my mother. On a day like this, it meant that the world beyond the three of us faded into the background, a little lilt on the air, a charming mumble.

All my boyhood memories of you are like this. A brief, suggestive interruption of a life I lived without you. We would meet. You would delight in your son. I would feel spoiled rotten, trying to soak up each moment together in all its detail. Then we would part. In the moments after, I would wail for want of you, before becoming quiet for days. My mother would worry for me as she navigated her own seas of love and hatred of you. Then the whole topic of "my father" would begin to fade from consciousness, sometimes for years. Most days, I lived as if you did not exist. It is only recently that I tried to think about what you were thinking then. Or what you felt that day.

I remember other little flashes of things about that trip to Ireland. I remember my mother, her mother, and I taking a ferry to one of the Aran Islands. We walked a five-mile stretch, and I tried to take seriously the charge a local man gave me to uncover the faeries there. He probably laughed at the predictable gullibility of Americans. But as my grandmother gingerly made her way over and through this green-and-gray labyrinth, the one that my mother assured her was the true repository of our nationality, I saw the faeries squelching in the mud near every low rock wall. I inhaled the briny Atlantic air, proud that unlike my classmates who called themselves Italian, I had put my Velcroed foot onto something solid on the opposite side of the Jersey shore. I remember later when a cab driver made the sign of the cross as we passed by the parish church. And my grandmother imitated him, having only just discovered this sign of devotion.

I remember being waist high to you and my mother in a crowded, dark pub somewhere, and the slightly renegade thrill of being in a place made for adults. I remember the way you ended your sentences with a suggestive "you know." To this boy's ears, it was an invitation to be with you in every story. "I was working in the black market, you know. When you were born, I went straight, you know. Not very much money, you know." My impertinent counting of the drinks each of you had was appraised as the work of America's antidrinking propaganda on the young. I remember the sound of Irish music enveloping us, that propulsive and occasionally annoying clatter of banjos, fiddles, and tin whistles. Beneath the harsh stage lights, and amidst the smell of cigarette smoke, watery stout, and mold somewhere in the building, there were men singing. And in my memory, the men singing and playing are transformed into the Irish folksingers my mother inflicted on me with her cassettes: Every baritone is Christy Moore. Every tenor, Paul Brady.

I had this dim sense of the two of you enjoying

each other, and enjoying me. I moved about this world in which every object was charged with meaning. I remember Mom's blue eye shadow and the gold-plated bangles and your thick Irish wool jumper. I remember that my mother's Virginia Slims suddenly had this new Irish name, "fags," which I was not allowed to repeat. I remember the smoke drifting up from her glass held at the height of my head, and seeming to curl around your arm like a lasso. And I was praying it would pull you two closer to each other.

But my prayers were not answered. And my memory turns back to America.

———

My mother had let her life be turned upside down by my birth. She lost her job at Toshiba, since an unwed mother was not acceptable to Japanese corporations at that time. She got another one at

IBM. Things were just tight enough that we still lived at her parents' home, where she slept on a sofa bed at night. Things were just flush enough that she could send me to Catholic school. She would come home late at night, in her smart work clothes, and I would lie on her arm, watching the light from the television glint off the edge of her little yellow-gold Cartier watch, before falling asleep with the smell of her Chanel No. 5 perfume in my nose.

My mother's side of the family left Ireland with the Great Famine still a fresh memory. But over a century later, in my boyhood home, my mother's parents had let the Irish and the hyphen gradually recede from their Irish-American identity. My grandparents had a few records of American crooners who put out albums of Irish tunes. My grandmother sang "Too-Ra-Loo-Ra-Loo-Ral," an "Irish lullaby" composed in Detroit. My grandfather had some glassware with our Anglicized last name, Dougherty, printed on it with a family crest.

It wasn't homesickness that burdened my mother with the idea of Ireland. It was her unrequited love for a real Irishman, yourself. Traveling Europe in the 1970s, she used her claim to Irishness to make friends, and to make love. Her best friend, an Irish Londoner, introduced you to her. You left her with a baby and then you continued on in the life you had before us.

She informed you of my birth by letter. Your brother, traveling through to Philadelphia, was the first of your family to even see me. You reconnected with an old girlfriend and made a family in Malahide. And in your absence—in her heartsickness—my own nursery was injected with a peculiar kind of Irish nationalism. My mother wanted me to know myself as Irish, and made her efforts.

She took me to the Irish culture festivals—

feiseanna—throughout New Jersey, where she collected little awards for singing old ballads and for her increasing proficiency in the Irish language. She wore a claddagh ring. She wore a green-and-gold bracelet for the release of political prisoners in Northern Ireland. She brought me to bars in Boston and put spare money into those woolen Irish flat caps when collections went out for the "widows and orphans" of West Belfast. She was smart enough to know what the money really was for.

Her love of Ireland was refreshed by waves of Irish men and women landing on the eastern seaboard in the 1980s. I can only barely remember some of the first names: Bobby. Trasa. Donal. We'd meet them in Queens, and with them she would curse the name of Margaret Thatcher. In my first years, she read me children's books in Irish. Nearly every night she put me to bed saying good night in Irish: "*Oíche mhaith.*" She took me away to what we called "Gaeltacht weekends" in sprawling and half-abandoned religious retreat houses. They had a rule: Try to speak only Irish. And there we would gather with other Irish people who were proving to themselves, at least, that there was still life in a dying language.

By the time I was a young adult I would know the history of Ireland well enough to debate it with friends and teachers. The story as I knew it was straightforward and heroic: a people coming out of captivity. There was colonization and misrule on one side, fitful Irish resistance on the other. Irish people launched periodic rebellions over the centuries: against Protestant usurpers; against misrule from Westminster; against wicked landlords; against the power of the old English monarchy; against British imperialism; against those who had attempted to rob them of their culture, their language, their land. It was as if rebellion itself made you Irish. The misrule culminated in the Great Famine and the waves of migration that sent one side of my ancestors to America and that nearly extinguished the nationhood of Ireland. The rebellions culminated and were fulfilled in the Easter Rising, the resurrection of the Irish nation.

The absurdly theatrical rebellion took Dublin as its stage on Easter Monday 1916 and began when a schoolteacher, Patrick Pearse, wearing a green military uniform in front of the General Post Office in Dublin, proclaimed an Irish Republic to passersby. The moment had been years in the making. When World War I had started, the Brits had suspended implementation of a Home Rule parliament in Ireland, then set about recruiting Irishmen to fight in the trenches so that the small nations of Europe might be free. Believing that "England's difficulty is Ireland's opportunity," a core of Irish nationalists decided instead to fight for the freedom of their own nation. The paramilitary Irish Volunteers, originally formed to defend Home Rule, would be deployed for a more ambitious purpose.

Pearse, and some of the Irish Volunteers with him, some of them only just informed they were part of a revolution, seized a handful of buildings and positions throughout Dublin. Less than a week later, after bloody street fighting with British troops rushed across the Irish Sea, and constant shelling from a gunship anchored in the River Liffey, the Rising ended in a humiliating military failure. Pearse handed his sword to British officers, and the rebels surrendered. The Republic lasted six days.

As its leaders were marched into prisons by British forces, they were cursed by the common people of Dublin as traitors and murderers. The Rising had wrecked the United Kingdom's second city, inspired looters, and resulted in the deaths of hundreds of Irish bystanders, some of them children. It temporarily stopped wives from getting the checks for their husbands' military service. It would soon result in mass arrests and even tighter wartime censorship. Not even two thousand Irish men and women had participated in the Rising, while over a hundred times that number of Irish men were fighting in British uniforms on the western front in the Great War. Pearse predicted in a letter to his mother from Kilmainham jail, "People will say hard things of us now, but we shall be remembered by posterity and blessed by unborn generations."

He was right. In those following days Ireland came to know the identity of the rebels—the schoolteacher Pearse, the journalist Seán Mac Diarmada, the language activist Éamonn Ceannt—and saw them as noble men. The British began executing them, one by one. They propped up the injured labor agitator James Connolly in a chair to shoot him. The poet Joseph Mary Plunkett, who drew up the war plans, married his sweetheart there in Kilmainham just before he was shot.

Dublin had been, for centuries, the seat of foreign rule. But now, christened by the blood of Irish patriots, it was redeemed. The martyrs became the heroes of a people's ballads, and the rebel cause won a posthumous mandate, inflaming the nation and setting twenty-six counties of Ireland on a course to full separation from Britain. Such was the power in this romantic, doomed yet successful, self-sacrifice.

Its power reached over the ocean and forward through time. Pearse and his friends shaped part of my childhood. What they had done informed my mother's commitment to the Irish language and her support for the IRA in Northern Ireland. Later in life, in sepia tones, they would be there as I drank watery stout at my local Irish pub.

But in my childhood, their stories, along with so many others that dissolved into legends, gave me a sense of Ireland being just barely over the horizon. As a child, when we took vacations to the Jersey shore, I would point out over the water, squint, and tell my mother I could see it.

———

A year or so after you gave me that hurl in Clare, you were visiting me. Another of these eruptions into my life. I showed you what a Nintendo was. I remember us walking around the cozy streets of Halcyon Park, with its one-way lanes and 1,200-square-foot American dreams crowding each other. You ordered steak well done at the restaurant, and then I did too. (I would order my steak this way for the next ten years. Damn you for that.) My mother told us about her adventures in her 1970s MGB. You told me all about my older cousin Darragh, whom I should meet someday. And then we all had a snowball fight.

Then came the day you were supposed to leave. Already, the pattern of these partings was established. You leave; I cry. Then my mother tries to pick up the pieces. For that much, I suppose we were all steeling ourselves. But this time you had news to deliver before you left for Newark Airport, and before I was supposed to go to school that morning. And it was this moment that my mother cited again and again in years to come as revealing the full measure of your stupidity, your selfish shortsightedness, and the price it extracted from me and from her.

I sat in my grandmother's rocking chair, dressed in the uniform of my Catholic school, gray slacks, a white dress shirt, and a maroon tartan tie. I stared down at my black shoes and across an expanse of blue carpet, to you in the seat across from me. And you told me news. Your wife was pregnant. (Your *wife!* I had let myself forget.) And so you were having a child soon. I was going to be a brother. Technically, half of one.

How was I a brother to someone who was not my mother's child? What did it mean to be a big brother to someone three thousand miles away? Was I going to be to them what Darragh was to me? A name placed on a relative I'd never see? Being a child, I could not even ask these questions. The one skill I had to deploy when talking to adults was intuiting the exact response they wanted to solicit from me, and giving it fully. But the strategy was failing in that moment. What did you want from me? What did my mother want? I was falling silent. I was crying. You had to get into the car and go. Neither of us got to see how hard this was on the other. In a few minutes, I would run out of the house, venturing halfway up Farrandale Avenue under the delusion that I would make it to school before neighbors returned me to where any seven-year-old child sobbing that way belongs: his home. But in that moment, you gave me a good-bye hug and a reassurance that you were still my father. And that nothing would change between us.

All I ever wanted was for things to change.

I had never thought any of it through until then. I didn't really know why you lived three thousand miles away, I just knew enough not to ask. But this announcement revealed to me the secret hope in my heart. Until this moment, I had imagined that one day you might sit down and announce that you had found a job in America. And so you would see me more often, and my mother too.

Living without you was normal. But when you were around, things seemed open ended. All the things I didn't quite understand made me think our family could be patched up. Your announcement revealed this hope in me by extinguishing it for good. For the first time, and from then on, I would never be deluded again. I would grow up a fatherless child. And nothing would change.

Years later my mother told me she had screamed at you in the car on the way to the airport. It should have been her to tell me, at the right time, she held. But you and I both know, in situations like this, there is no right time. There is just the news.

Up until then, my mother might have let me draw you a doodle and include it in a letter back to you. Or even sign my name to a birthday card. Up until this time, I remembered some talk of me coming to join you in Ireland, by myself, in the summer months. All the little markings in the letters, all the talk of a more proper relationship between father and son was now at an end. My mother would put ideas to me as objectively as she could. I could go and stay with you there if I liked. I shouldn't worry for her but give my own answer.

But my ability to give the solicited response would not fail here. How could I leave the woman who stayed with me? How could I leave the woman whose life, I was coming to believe, was ruined for my own sake? I was the man of the house, from then on.

Nearly a quarter of a century later, on another gray day in Ireland, you and I were together again, this time in working-class Finglas. It was then, in my early thirties, with my wife using her phone to photograph us, that I watched my first hurling match. Twenty-five years from the time a hurl was put into my hand, until I stood on the pitch. It took me twenty-five years to discover that the blue stripe near the bas on my childhood hurl was the blue of your Dublin team. In the same time, I had only seen hurling as a snippet in a famous Guinness commercial, while you had spent some time almost every week following the local club. And in all that time in America, none of the many substitute father figures in my life, my uncles or teachers, came and put an ash baseball bat in my hands.

We stood there in the light rain in Finglas and we watched a match together, shuffling backward and forward toward the edge of the soggy pitch, watching the players run through the rain. Their hurls raised, as if in some kind of ancient form of combat. Once a *sliotar* was airborne, a man would instantly smash it downfield toward the hand of a jumping teammate, who, in one smooth motion, returns to the ground, tosses it in front of his body, slips through a clatter of hurls defending against him, and then blasts it with his own, sending it fifty yards through the air and between the goal-posts. My wife drew my attention to the fact that you and I hold ourselves the same way. When we put our hands on our hips, we unconsciously point our thumbs forward. Almost everyone else on earth holds their hands the opposite way. It was

easy to enjoy the action, and the interested mur-
muring on the sidelines, and our sense of close-
ness. But within a few minutes, the entire distance
of the Atlantic Ocean opened up between us again.
The instant a *sliotar* fell into the hand of a man
well positioned in front of the goal, you shouted
"Bury it," in your Dublin accent. An instant later,
an instant too late, I would let out a very American "C'mon!" Two feet apart and twenty-five
years separating us. I had no feel for this game, for
its rhythm, its clashing sounds and terrifying
speed. Sport—the very thing that made it easy for
almost any other two men to find ease and com-
monality with each other—reminded me instantly
that in your presence I am family, but still un-
familiar. I am proximate, nowhere near close.

I felt on the edge of the pitch that if I was Irish
at all, it was only in the most technical and bureau-
cratic sense. The Irish state, recognizing the circumstances of my birth, must give me a passport

and allow me to live and work in Ireland if I choose. If I came, a week after all the Irish people give me their charming and clichéd "Welcome home," the same Irish people would be obliged to dismiss me as a "blow-in."

At that hurling pitch in Finglas, I would have said my mother's great effort was in vain. What was my Irishness? It was my pedantic correction to those who say "Saint Patty's Day" rather than "Paddy's Day." It was my mother's drum, the *bodhran*, under my bed, unplayed in years. It was my overfamiliarity with these men of the Rising on the walls of O'Connor's Public House on Route 22 in Brewster, New York. It was an accident, reinforced only by my Irish last name, which created the expectation that I should be interested in and knowledgeable about Ireland.

Because I was raised apart from you, my Irishness has to be self-consciously asserted or it ceases to exist in me. My siblings, who grew up in your home, could be or do anything and some residue of Irishness would stick to them and to all they do. It is their accent and their memories. It's in the story their American and English employers tell about them. It's the smile of recognition that creeps across their face when their friend rolls his eyes at another "Dub" who helplessly reveals himself as a Northsider or a Southsider.

I, on the other hand, am what many Irish people would call a plastic Paddy. A Yank. A tourist who stumbles on a ruined castle and thinks it's the old family homestead, then babbles about how good the Guinness is wherever I happen to land in Ireland, when, objectively, the Guinness there is a bit shit.

And there is something else to contend with. To even consider Ireland a nation is to invite a sneer from her most privileged citizens. We're all supposed to know that it is something else: a thing the British invented out of a hodgepodge of anarchic clans and a smattering of leftover Vikings, a fiction that we now see through, a dodgy tax shelter robbing the EU. All nations are in some way dissolving, we're told, and that the dissolution is a good thing. Ireland's national pride is a font of violence, a spur to extremism and superstition. And besides, Ireland is a failure. It has always been a failure. After all, my ancestors left. James Joyce left. Ireland's children still leave. They send back selfies from Bondi Beach in Sydney. They send back money from Vancouver. They leave for better climate. They leave for jobs. They leave to escape the gombeen men, the swish of the soutane, and the stony gray soil.

I have to laugh. They all leave, but you stayed.

———

A few weeks ago, it was my turn to make an announcement: My wife is pregnant with your first grandchild. My half sisters just had brunch with us in New York, and they relayed your prediction, made upon hearing the news: "He's going to get into his roots." You are already right. That very week, a question had fallen on me. What songs should I sing to my daughter when she comes? It occurred to me that in a few months I would have this life wriggling across my lap. I would have to tell her who she is. The question left something in me changed, changed utterly.

I am suddenly alive to the idea that I could pass on this immense inheritance of imagination and passion if only I could work up the courage to claim it for myself. After that brunch, I ordered a dozen children's books in Irish. Ahem, *as Gaeilge*. Many of them are the books I had in childhood. I bought an Irish dictionary. I've been collecting books about the Rising. And relearning the songs that inspired it, making a mental catalogue of the ones that were suitable for lullabies. I'm sure it all looks crazy.

I know that when I try to assert this Irish thing, it seems soapy, "Oirish," or just hopelessly quixotic. But I do not lack for company. The men of the Easter Rising had backgrounds that made them self-conscious and assertive about their Irishness. Tom Clarke's father served in the British Army. Patrick Pearse had a slight Birmingham accent, inherited from his father. Éamon de Valera, born in New York City, was ridiculed as a half-Spanish bastard. All on account of their fathers. I've come to think that these men have something to tell me in this moment, as I become a father.

This child, my child, is coming presently, and I am determined not to withhold any part of my heart from her. And I need to be fully present to her. I feel this invigorating need to be stronger and better than I have been. That my manhood is at stake. And if there is an inheritance to be had in being Irish, I will recover it for her. And I need you for both of these missions.

All my life, save for a few weeks, has been spent an ocean away from you. Now, for this child's sake, I hope to bridge that gap. It means finding a way back to each other, doesn't it? And for me it also means asserting the Irish thing, the way my mother did.

How did we get to that field in Finglas, looking like father and son, but sounding like foreigners to one another? How did I come to this desperate feeling of wanting to recover all these artifacts of Irish nationalism, at the very minute Irish people are happy to throw them away? Sometimes I get the sense that the moment we catch a serious emotion our temptation as men—as Irishmen?—is to do what your man did with the *sliotar*: bury it. And there still is something unsaid between us.

Your son,
Michael

II

Putting Childish Things Away

The modern Irish, contrary to popular impression,
have little sense of history. What they have is a
sense of grievance, which they choose to dignify
by christening it history.

—*J. J. Lee*

Dear Father,

It wasn't long after you gave me the news about my baby-sister-to-be that you began to cut my mother out as our go-between. You would address your letters to me directly. You would update me on my sister. Then my sisters, plural. And finally inform me of my impending little brother. From your perspective, I'm sure it seemed like the minimum you must do. You never once disclaimed me as your son. But by this point, I was disclaiming you.

The next time I saw you was in 1994 and I was wearing the exact same outfit as on that day I wept on Farrandale Avenue. The tartan tie, the short-sleeved white shirt, and the gray pants had all been ordered from yellow sheets of paper, in larger and larger sizes, year after year. These were the final days of my sixth grade, my final ones in uniform as a Catholic-school boy. Mom's job had moved to Westchester, and we were moving with it.

I was sitting at my lunch table when a friend drew my attention to a stranger peeking in through the door from the hallway. You stood out easily among the students in uniforms and nuns in habits. One of those nuns came over to the table and informed me that you were waiting to see me. I tossed my bologna sandwich into a garbage can, and there you were. It had been three years, and suddenly you were here again, without warning.

We were invited out into the huge expanse of pavement that was my place for recess. I can remember talking to you out there, while the principal watched us from the door. Bells rang and classes restarted, but we stayed out there. You gave me a white-and-green shirt, with Saint Patrick on it, celebrating Ireland's participation in the World Cup, here in America. You were going to see the match against Italy at Giants Stadium. And then after a few minutes you were gone.

I went back in and joined my classmates in the duties of the last days of the Catholic school year, cleaning our own classrooms. Everyone asked me about you. "Your dad? Really?" "From Ireland? Really?" Some envied me the privilege of not seeing my father for years on end. I was tempted to agree with them.

It was a bright, balmy day. The sky was streaked in tangerine when school let out. Normally I might have taken the public bus home. Today, I walked and thought. Who were you, anyway? You were the man who showed up every few years. The man who wrote me letters about the latest developments in his household, the home in which I played no role.

You were what my mother reminded me you were: not here for me. You were not here a summer earlier, when a wild-eyed man running along Bloomfield Avenue punched me in the head. You weren't there when the winter before that I had suffered two concussions in a week, and my mother endured the horror of knowing her only son was being hospitalized while she sat in traffic on the Tappan Zee Bridge. You weren't there when I had to overcome being the boy in class who got teased constantly. You might have taught me to be brave or stoic. Or perhaps your presence in my life would have given me a confidence that warded off this treatment.

I turned up Parkway West and saw that Mom's car was in front of the house. Why was she home early? Maybe we were all going to get dinner. I put the keys in the door. And there she was, relieved to see me. She had rushed home when the nuns informed on your sudden presence. It turned out that it wasn't just a meeting without warning for me, but one without authorization from her. She hugged me, asking me what took me so long getting home, and telling me how she worried I might be on a plane, kidnapped and heading for Dublin. I was asked to debrief her on every detail of the encounter.

Once the story was established to her satisfaction, she put you on a kind of trial. The facts: You came and saw me. But obviously you were in America for other purposes. Namely, the World Cup. And seeing a friend in Philadelphia. Couldn't I see that adding your son to the list made a better and more noble cover story with your wife, for what amounted to a getaway to Giants Stadium with your friend?

I put that St. Patrick's World Cup shirt in my drawer and never wore it. But my mother and I talked about it. We told ourselves a story that the Irish had printed it up in a foolish and oh-so-Irish belief that qualifying for the World Cup destined them to win it. We told ourselves that you bragged about your son in the pubs back home, but my mother was stuck with all the real work. It was in stories like these, the stories I told myself, that I was gathering the strength to put you out of mind for my teenage years.

I was putting Ireland itself out of my mind too. Or trying to, and it wasn't hard to dismiss it, since the Irish "thing" was changing for us here. Ireland for me had been the boyhood weekends with Irish-language revivalists, or with the sad drunk émigrés in Queens. It was frivolously contributing to NORAID, and being dimly and stupidly proud of the mayhem the word "Irish" seemed to carry in it.

By September 1994, there was a ceasefire in Northern Ireland. And this development seemed to change everything. My mother, without ever feeling a need to explain the apparent change in her politics, was singing along to the Cranberries and their tuneful denunciations of the Provisional IRA, as we unloaded boxes in our new townhouse in Putnam County, New York. The flat caps were no longer passed around for widows and orphans. The whole social constellation that revolved around Irish America's version of Irish nationalism was falling apart. At least for us. Our sense of Ireland no longer came from these little retreat houses and Queens bars. Many of the Irish emigrants themselves went back home as the economy started to pick up. Irishness now came out of public television, the enormous new bookstores and movie theaters popping up along Interstate 84. It wasn't people, but stuff, this cultural flotsam coming across the ocean and being sold to us.

We had a CD by a Canadian Irish group, the Rankin Family, playing endlessly, along with Enya and Black 47. Soon it was the Corrs, and more experimental stuff by Sinead O'Connor. In the following year, there was Michael Flatley's Riverdance, passing quickly from Eurovision to American PBS and into semiconstant rotation on our VCR. Tim Pat Coogan's book *The Troubles* came out and so did Thomas Cahill's *How the Irish Saved Civilization*. One of my cousins denounced it as "ethnic essentialism," and thank God she did. At the time I'd take anything to relieve me from the Irish.

Ireland was also turning into a kind of New Age symbol, one being sold out of the tiny incense shops you'd find in vacation towns in New England. Reconnect with your roots. Get a tattoo of Celtic knots, then reinvigorate your soul through Irish paganism. Let the wisdom of ancient Druids save you from your lame legalistic sacraments and deliver you to knowledge of your chakras, or whatever. It all fits in with the enlightened Eastern traditions, and the insights of astrology, we were told, and sometimes we pretended to believe it. We never took it seriously, though we did stop going to church. Irishness alone allowed us to claim spirituality on the cheap.

You would send me more clothes with the word Ireland printed on them—I remember a jacket you sent for Christmas. I never wore it. The way to fit in with my friends was to wear a puffy New Jersey Devils Starter jacket. You sent me a dual CD of Irish folk legend Luke Kelly's greatest hits. I shelved it and never listened to it. I preferred Boyz II Men. My extended family bought tickets to see Riverdance at Radio City Music Hall, and I at least pretended to find it tedious.

What was Ireland, beyond this tidal wave of consumable stuff crashing through our home? In the 1990s Ireland was retelling its own stories to itself, in the belief that it was finally coming into its own. Perhaps because Irish identity seemed more and more like a commodity, something touched up and sold to the world, the Irish wanted to be unsentimental and undeluded about their history. Somehow turning Ireland into a product for consumption by the diaspora and the rest of the world allowed the Irish to take stock of themselves. As usual, they found themselves wanting.

Revisionism hardly begins to describe the way Ireland's national story was demolished and rebuilt. Irish historians speculated that Patrick Pearse was erotically attracted to the boys of his school, putting at least the hint of child abuse at the beginning of Ireland's story. Irish journalists chased after World War I veterans, telling us they'd been unjustly neglected in favor of the Easter Rising. Thirty years of the IRA campaign in Ulster had had an effect, and those who detested modern Sinn Fein were firm in their resolve to tear down the national mythology that inspired the "men of violence." With this came a renewed scrutiny of Ireland's postindependence institutions, the mother and baby homes, industrial schools, and the Magdalene laundries. Liam Neeson played Michael Collins in the movie, and he was sainted in it, not because of his innovations in urban guerrilla warfare, but because he was willing to stand behind an imperfect compromise with Great Britain. How on the mark for the time! My boyhood understanding of Irish history, a people coming out of captivity, now got a chuckle from serious historians. They informed us in their soft Dublin accents, "We're all revisionists now."

You yourself share in the prevailing Irish attitude of our time. You tell me that Ireland was a "dark" country until just recently. Nothing open. Nothing going on. The food was poor. How the Church lorded it over everyone. Explaining it to me, in generalities, you even pulled your coat tighter to symbolize the chill you felt just thinking about the place. Now Ireland had a real nightlife. There was more opportunity for jobs. You could get divorced now, which could make getting married in the first place a bit easier. Beneath this, I got the sense that the falling price of travel had made Irish life easier on the Irish, who were, in Yeats's phrase, "a worldwide Nation, always growing Sorrow!"

The demolition job on old Ireland and its nationalist myths certainly rhymed with my own life, which at that time was thick with skepticism for everything received. Even as a teenager I could feel this sense of boundlessness and abundance; this giddy feeling that there were almost no limits to what I could do, that I was bounding forward on an ever-increasing standard of living. And what good could come from zealotry? Absolute claims in religion and politics always ended in disaster, didn't they? What you had to do was to slip through the already loose grip of taboos and superstitions of the past, and the world was at your feet.

And we were already well on our way. The faeries were back in the muck somewhere in the Aran Islands, irrelevant. Religion was a pastime for those who wanted or needed something to do, but there was plenty to be done. The men of the Rising were intransigent fanatics in their day, and transformed by death into tyrants over the present. It was as if there were an all too obvious lesson in the air. In America the peace dividend translated into a long boom. We now lived in new construction, a townhouse more than twice the size of my childhood home. In Ireland the ceasefire in the North helped make the conditions for a Celtic Tiger economy. You expanded your house, too.

Now was the time to be preoccupied with the important things: obtaining good grades, filling out a suitable roster of extracurricular activities. Activity itself was good enough, no need for actual achievements. These would yield acceptance to a good college and the very successful life that was obviously just on the other side of any degree. And you even gave me a foretaste of this yourself. Your letters came to me still, and in the most mercenary way, I looked forward to them.

Cutting my mother out resulted in a peace dividend for me. For every birthday and for Christmas, you wrote a fat check made out to me personally. The very unofficial arrangement of child support became something more like child indulgence. I can't remember many of the stories you relayed in these letters, but even now twenty years later I can recall the typical amounts filled in on the checks. None of us were rich, by the standards of even our own towns, but these were fat times. These checks, and the sense of prosperity around us, made it feel like I was being let in on the great facts of the adult world. What matters is bread on the table. Ireland had a pretty iffy record as an independent nation, but it was unbeatable as a brand for products. We had put away the foolish fairy tales about ourselves, and now we told a story about prosperity.

———

Telling a story at all changes your relationship to the events you are describing. My mother and I, in trying to deny how helpless we sometimes felt, distorted the stories we told each other about you. She and I let our emotional needs twist the truth. Perhaps I'm doing the same thing now in my desire to connect with my roots. Nations can do the same thing. Some of the mythology that grew around the Rising obviously served to rally and moralize the Irish through the difficulties and trials of establishing the independence proclaimed by the heroes of 1916. But priorities change. The great imperative twenty-five years ago was peace on the island, so the Irish told stories that down-played the militancy of Irish nationalism. Now the imperative is inclusion, so the story conveniently omits the stuff about nation and sacrifice and loyalty.

Let's grant for a moment that we are all revisionists now. That we all retell stories in light of our motives. The next question would be: What are your motives? What does this retold story do to the people hearing it, or to the person telling it? If we want noble things in life, we will pull those noble things out of our history and experience. If we are cynics, we will see plenty of justification for our cynicism.

A false motive might produce a false history, something Ireland has seen plenty of. There were the antiquarians who believed the Irish language came unscathed from Babel. There is the false nationalist history in which all the invasions of Ireland were crimes of the English. Some older Irish people I've run into will recall with surprise the moment they learned that the Normans, who invaded in 1169, spoke a form of French. They were shocked to learn that Pope Alexander III essentially deeded Ireland to King Henry II.

Then there is the false history of Ireland imposed by the English, a kind of nonhistory. In it, Ireland is merely a tangle of rude peoples waiting for English intervention, for English invention of the Irish. And no one thanked them for it.

Have you noticed how modern Irish pols talk about Ireland's past whenever an important English person is thought to be in earshot? They rely on clichés about "our tangled history" or "our shared history." Maybe that is expedient. But it's false. Sharing was not the intention of the English or the Irish until very, very recently. Ireland's modern history began not with persuasion and unity but with plunder.

This robbery was not just the seizure of land, it was an attempt to take from the Irish their ability to define or know themselves, to confiscate their language, their culture, even their character. When the English were not expropriating Irish wealth and murdering Irish people, they were Anglicizing them, making them believe that they should be grateful for the intervention. This vision of Irish incompetence is internalized in many Irish minds to this day. In many ways, it provides the emotional motor for those revisionists who make grand pronouncements about how Ireland is nothing but a failure. To rebel against England, an Irishman first rebels against this lie.

An outstanding example of such a rebel is Eoin MacNeill, a professor and leader of the Irish Volunteers whose own story has been distorted by political ambitions. He's been made a false villain by Irish republicans for his order to delay the Rising. He's sometimes been championed falsely as a hero of peace for the same. The truth is that Eoin MacNeill, both as scholar and rebel, recovered for the Irish the dignity of their own history.

MacNeill was born in 1867, making him older than most of the other men involved in the Rising. As a professor of Early Irish History at the new University College Dublin, he uncovered the story of a Gaelic civilization that waxed as continental Europe went into its Dark Age. He did not brag outrageously, as Thomas Cahill does, that the Irish saved civilization, but it is impossible to imagine Cahill's bragging without MacNeill's work. His training in the language gave him the ability to do the forensic work of tying together Ireland's collections of genealogies with its collections of annals.

The story he found was not one of bumbling failure. MacNeill documented the fact that while the Roman Empire collapsed on the Continent, and gave way to fledgling Germanic states, Gaelic civilization flourished in Ireland. It developed a post-Latin literature in the Irish language well ahead of other European languages. Religious men who spoke and wrote in Irish founded monasteries as far away as Mainz in Germany and Bobbio in Italy. MacNeill, almost singlehandedly, had debunked the Irish legend-tellers. The sentimental stories, the ones that made a good product, could be set aside, and replaced with something better, something real.

What strikes me about MacNeill is the sheer energy behind his toiling, and his ability to resist these mysteriously twinned temptations. To despair of his nation's history, or to turn it into some cheap product. He traveled the country giving lectures on Irish history. He founded an Irish language printing press business in 1902, and suffered heavy losses with it. He was a journalist, contributing work to several societies dedicated to Ireland's cultural and Gaelic renaissance at the turn of the century.

That was his response to the robbery of Ireland: tireless work. He did not lie about the past for reasons of propaganda, like some of his co-revolutionaries did. He did not let the bleakness one finds in history cause him to indulge in self-dramatized despair. He worked to describe Ireland to itself, to recover its memory, and to recover its language. He is as much a national hero as any man who fought in the Rising.

MacNeill's enemy was not just the English, of course, but the lassitude of the Irish. This is one of the least understood aspects about political nationalism, and I'm surprised this misunderstanding could even grow up in Ireland. Nationalism usually does not spring from the meatheaded conviction that one's nation is best in every way, but from something like a panicked realization that nobody in authority or around you is taking the nation seriously, that everyone is engaged in some private enterprise, while the common inheritance is being threatened or robbed. It might put on a mask of invincibility, but it does so in full fearful knowledge of the nation's vulnerability.

MacNeill never put down his books while pursuing a greater level of self-understanding for his nation. And this, in turn, meant that when the time came, he found himself ready to lead men who might one day fight for Ireland's freedom. He was able to warn his compatriots against letting slogans do their thinking for them, and criticized those who were "really impelled by a sense of . . . fatalism, or by an instinct of satisfying their own emotions, or escaping from a difficult and complex and trying situation."

Was MacNeill's story of Ireland motivated? Yes, it was. But he somehow resisted the temptation to let his desires and psychological needs fatally distort his perception. Instead he tries to get to the truth as best he can. And this attempt to recover an accurate understanding of his nation, and his place in its history, doesn't paralyze him, but makes him all the more willing to act and to act bravely.

He is an example for our age, I think, and for us personally. As I try to plumb our history in these letters, I don't want to give in to despair on the one side, or an undemanding sentimentality on the other. We cannot help but bring our desires and our ambitions to our understandings, and so I think the only solution is to make sure we desire what is right and good.

Since I've begun considering the problem of revision and motivation, I've been going through my mother's old letters to you. Each one contains this remarkable and brave performance. She would start with the updates, the news. Michael is on to this or that. And then she would lay into you. She would explain, in vivid detail, how every arrangement you proposed, every gesture you offered, was inadequate to the situation at hand. But then, before she came to the end, she would shift her tone. She tried to morally coerce you into "giving it a shot," because you owed it to me. At the same time, she would distill her anger into something more fragrant, a hint at a depth of feeling she still had for you. Your curse was in being so easy to love.

Over the years, I notice she shifted to warning you to keep a distance. It was too hard for me, she said, to have a father drop in once every few years. But in truth she was protecting herself as well. And, noticing her feelings, I recruited myself into the project, giving you years of stony silence.

How will we explain this curious detail about our lives to your grandchild when she comes into this world? How will she come to understand that one grandfather lives twenty minutes up the road and is there in every picture of his daughter's life, while another granddad lives three thousand miles away and has left so little trace in his son's life beyond a great pile of words? Your letters, which contain the updates on your household, your thoughts on the passing seasons. Like MacNeill, I've learned to decode this wealth of documented evidence. And I'm afraid that I had it all wrong, that these letters, which I once passed over so casually, brim with longing—longing for me—just as my mother's did for you. That is our history.

Your son,
Michael

III

Who Made Me

For men improve with the years;
And yet, and yet,
Is this my dream, or the truth?
O would that we had met
When I had my burning youth!

—W. B. Yeats, *"Men Improve with the Years"*

Dear Father,

We feel like we are getting to know this child already, the way she turns over or dances for us as the doctor shakes her awake to observe her on the ultrasound. I had this fear that she would look up at me, and I would be charged with telling her who she was. I'm starting to realize that the fear is hotter the other way. I fear she will look up at me, and I will helplessly reveal who I am, with all my faults becoming plainer to her each day.

We're in for it, they tell us, about parenthood. We are getting tired of everyone warning us that the struggles of a new baby will leave us so tired. War metaphors abound. Other parents are "veterans" on their way back from the front lines. An adorable tiny rocking hammock is recast as "the essential weapon" to deploy. If it's a battle to raise a child, we need reinforcements.

I suppose you get reinforcement. Not only extended family and friends, but the larger culture raises and forms your children, whether you'd want it or not. A home is a refuge, but it still sits within something larger, a homeland, or a culture. In your absence, my mother had given me this familiarity with Ireland's story and the high ideals of its national history. And then, this larger culture around her, and I began to deconstruct that story, and it nudged me along in efforts to deconstruct it as well. Deconstruction of this sort was just the thing to do.

A culture is a funny thing. Somehow it is this collective personality that is constantly feeding you information about itself. It ranks and reranks everything in life—people, objects, and ideas. It turns articles of clothing into symbols of high or low status. It suggests certain ideas and dismisses others. Its judgments become so familiar that it exists like a voice in your head. And yet it is impossible to explain exactly how this happens.

A culture feeds you even the terms on which you would resist it. The culture that encouraged us to deconstruct the ideals and taboos of Ireland's past because, as Ireland's former Taoiseach John Bruton put it, they have "an unhealthy hold upon the living" was the same culture that told me that by doing so, by doing what everyone else was doing, we were defining life on our own terms, and for ourselves.

So what were our background cultures? Our boyhoods could not have been more different. You had five siblings and two parents at home. You grew up in a tight two-up, two-down in Donnycarney and the streets had hundreds of children in them. The schools that were built to handle this were called "industrial." One of the most infamous of these, Artane, cast its shadow into your neighborhood. In summers you were sent to your grandparents in Monaghan, to avoid the training in criminality available just out your door. Fathers were deputized by God to rule their homes. The Catholic Church of your youth was a spiritual empire, sending Irish emissaries across the sea. It spoke Latin, threw incense generously, and ran the world as you knew it, because the unquenchable fire of hell burbled beneath everything. People you knew would be genuinely afraid of receiving Holy Communion unworthily.

The heroes of the Easter Rising were still venerated as saints. When you were a child, Ireland's president and a hero of the rebellion laid a wreath at the jail where his comrades were condemned to death and killed. The life of the nation was serious business. The adult world throbbed with authority and frequently abused it. Maybe Ireland would be poor, but it would be sanctified and creative. This was what one of Ireland's leading writers calls the myth of Holy Catholic Ireland, a myth that shaped your childhood. A myth that Ireland has spent the last three decades dismantling. The last artifacts of it are eagerly chucked away.

That world was as distant from mine as medieval France is. I grew up an only child with a single mother. I lived in a series of American suburbs, one seemingly more prosperous than the next. There were dozens of kids in the neighborhoods, not hundreds, and nothing as exciting as criminality. The Church was a friendly ghost. Nobody feared approaching for Communion. God would be merciful, surely. If you were unusually curious and asked about the apparent change of attitude, you would be assured that many theologians thought Hell was empty.

When I was a child the nation's president disclosed to us his preference in underwear for a laugh. The adult world that I encountered was plainly terrified of having authority over children and tried to exercise as little of it as practicable. At every turn my mother, my teachers, and the Church just sort of gave up and gave in to whatever I wanted. They seemed grateful when a child wasn't difficult. The constant message of authority figures was that I should be true to myself. I should do what I loved, and I could love whatever I liked. I was the authority. In the benighted past somewhere, there was pain and misery, but baby boomers had largely corrected this for us in their titanic generational battles. This, I would call the myth of liberation. I was raised on this mythology, and it ordered the world around me. The future ought to be bright. This was the end of history, and wasn't it good?

There was a mystery about the new townhouse development we had moved into, the one in the exurbs of Putnam County, New York. On the surface, what had seemed new, clean, and large slowly revealed itself as cheaper and draftier than we expected. But there was something else about it that began to weigh on me. Why build row houses in the middle of clear fields? Why build this enclosed, half-private, half-public green space? Soon I noticed that the classmates who moved into our development did so after their parents divorced. And then it became clearer to me. These houses were built to lean on each other because the homes inside were broken. The manicured green spaces between them gave kids places to play, but no way to walk to another neighborhood. The men who mowed our common green space, and the men who shoveled the stoops and the walkways, were all hired hands. These men themselves were thousands of miles from their children. This was an architecture of fatherlessness.

On the whole, your generation successfully minimized its own risk of becoming domestic tyrants. But they had done so by handing us over to ourselves, and many of us discovered the tyrant within. To empower me and my generation, everyone pretended that there were no insurmountable obstacles in the way of our finding our true selves. But this gave us the sense that every misfortune or setback was entirely self-authored. Assured there was no judgment from without, our desires and expectations made us pitiless judges of our own lives. We had little resilience to meet challenges; we assumed the adults would just keep removing them and settling things for us. But the message was still clear to us: Your parents had torn down almost all the unjust taboos and barriers.

You just needed a good education, and life would be whatever you wanted it to be. I believed this. It was so much a part of my mother's milk and the culture's propaganda that I have always struggled to disbelieve it, even now.

Because for a time, it seemed to work. As a teenager, wherever I wanted to go, a friend's car would arrive and take me there. Whenever I needed permission, it was given. High school teachers had decided I was intelligent and engaged in class, so they stopped marking me down for not doing homework. They asked politely that I do show up for class. My mother, practiced in years of indulging me, did the same. I was constantly in love, and the girls I loved returned love to me generously. No one expressed any worry about what kind of man this would make me. By all the measures that mattered, I was doing fine. Fatherless? Look at the grades. The world yielded to me, and in turn I would yield to it. To be young, dumb, and handsome enough. Looking back, I guess that was your excuse once too.

At the spiritual level, this myth of liberation—a liberation already accomplished—made my generation into powerless narcissists. We who worshipped authenticity—being your true self—even as most of us accused ourselves, in our own hearts, of being frauds. Some of us fell into despair and chemical dependency. Others coped through dual membership in the cults of productivity and self-care. A few now turn to internet father figures who tell them that life is struggle, that it is defined by self-assertion and dominance. And some, tired of trying to find a motive for existence from within, turned to political radicalism. But all this wreckage was a decade or more away from me and my friends then. We had no idea what was coming. Depression? Economically, we were assured it was unlikely to ever come again. Personally? Well, there were new drugs for it.

And my mother was increasingly on those drugs. When my grandmother died, my mother lost her role as the dutiful daughter. And she could see that in a few years I would also fly from home. Where would it leave her? I experienced the 1990s as me coming into my own, of the world opening up for me. My mother experienced something else. Her life shrunk. She didn't travel as much. She tried to make arrangements to move us to London, where she had been so happy once. But she shelved them.

There was a great deal of talk at that time about the heroism of single mothers, but not all the taboos were pulled down. She had stuck it out with the baby, assured that the world would increasingly accept, and admire, her decision. In truth, it did so only provisionally. IBM would not and then could not fire her for being a single mother. But her form of life as mother, often over-worked due to her circumstances, had none of the honor and understanding that is extended to widows, whom everyone feels obliged to help generously. This state of life was what she chose, after all. Or people would retain the suspicion that she must be at fault somehow, that she had failed to keep the man for a reason. Her form of being single was impaired by motherhood, having none of the real freedom and allure of those who were truly unattached. I would later discover she had admirers and even lovers, but she could—or would—never make them into committed boy-friends or suitors.

As depression set in, she gained weight and be-came more frequently ill. I heard people worry for her, saying that she was "letting herself go." She was. She lived on the other side of the culture's liberation, and her unhappiness in life was held to be her fault. The cliché about lying in the bed you have made for yourself became her reality. She had finally thrown away the old couch and pullout for a real, proper, queen-size bed. But now she slept in it constantly. It was as if the culture had slipped her its real judgment in secret, the cruel truth that was unspeakable in public. And she accepted that judgment and internalized it.

———

This larger cultural formation, as I received it, wasn't cruel to me. And although it had encouraged skepticism and deconstruction of anything received, it didn't take away everything of my childhood, exactly. It didn't vacate the world of all meaning, or make me a nihilist, living entirely in my own head. I still had an identity. People still joked about my 180-proof Irish name. I still needed meaning and purpose. And I still needed father figures. It didn't deny me these things outright, but it subtly changed their meaning.

Instead, it encouraged a curator's approach to life, which I took to be common among my friends. There was nothing that we were *obliged* to believe. No type of life that was strenuously urged on us. We could make use of our ethnic identities or not. We could draw on or reject our parent's religion, or be coolly indifferent. We could try on any number of identities. We could throw ourselves into a social scene, or, if you had skill, flit between them. The important thing was that it be entirely a personal choice. And, if you were talented, that you didn't screw up your earning potential in the future.

For white kids in the suburbs, paradoxically, this assumed freedom made the project of self-definition seem epic and unimportant at the same time. You were captain of your own ship, and you must chart some great adventure—but if there were no obstacles, how could you know the adventure was great? In some ways, I would have appreciated more pushback from my mother, from teachers, and from the culture. If only to give my acceptance of their guidance, or my rejection, some weight. And yet, I was happy.

Late in high school I grew close to an English teacher, Mr. Scanlon. He was the most important in a long succession of substitute father figures. He sprang around the halls of my school as if his movements were choreographed by an unseen animator. He was giving me the power of English, at least with a pen. In the long run, I suppose, he was giving me a livelihood. He was also a man with Irish roots. Knowing my background, he began feeding my imagination with W. B. Yeats, the Pogues, and James Joyce. "Who goes with Fergus?" he asked as he bounded into a room. He played "Bottle of Smoke" while we edited the school's literary magazine, and he filled my world with sad, colorful *Dubliners*.

I remember him reading out of Joyce, aloud, and an image from the short story "Araby" so impressed itself on my mind, it made its way into one of the many love letters I wrote as a young man. It's the one in which a young man obsesses over a woman he sees framed in the light of an open door. That little light, described by Joyce as shining out onto the darkened North Richmond Street in a Dublin winter, added color to my already colorful world. In a way, the clatter of Irish music, the strangeness of the Irish sky, and a repository of Ireland's national genius were all returned to me, not as an inheritance to be treasured and passed on, but as ornaments of a life defined by enjoyment, consumption. And this curator's approach seemed to let me enjoy them safely. That little bit of ironic distance prevented these things from really touching the parts of my soul and mind that were vulnerable to developing a deep conviction.

In all my reading, I've started to question whether the Irish are telling the whole truth about the Holy Catholic Ireland of the twentieth century. The Catholic Church in Ireland is so reduced, it has maybe half a dozen public apologists these days. They complain, sometimes tirelessly, of the unremittingly hostile media environment. They occasionally romanticize another Ireland. But I've been somewhat surprised to find that this perception— unremitting hostility against the Church—is not relatively new. It's older than you are.

In the first half of the 1950s, the poet Patrick Kavanagh wrote a parody of what we now take as the modern Dublin view of the world. "House Party to Celebrate the Destruction of the Roman Catholic Church in Ireland" takes the perspective of a man celebrating his spouse's new book. All the same rhetoric that we think of as modern

Ireland's clichés are present in the 1950s. In the poem, a husband is profoundly outraged that some "rural savage" has described his wife as "A female replica of Cromwell's face." And in his mind he retorts that "The Jansenistic priesthood of the nation / Had perished by this woman writer's hand." Something is so familiar about the following lines:

> The reviews were coming in by every post,
> Warm and fulsome – Seamus read extracts:
> 'The Roman Catholic Hierarchy must
> Be purple now with rage. She states the
>   facts
>
> With wit, and wit is what they cannot bear.'
> In far of parishes of Cork and Kerry
> Old priests walked homeless in the winter
>   air
> As Seamus poured another pale dry sherry.

I almost feel ashamed to say that I sympathize with the rural savage. As a teenager, I returned to the Church of my baptism. And also in an odd form and from an unlikely source. One of those girls who loved me was an Evangelical Christian. Her father and the other men of her church subverted my prejudices about enthusiastic Prods. My view had always been that American Baptists were, well, inherently ridiculous. But these were serious men, who thought hard and studied harder, not just on how to get ahead, but on how to live in this world, and how to love the people around them. They were impressive, and my teenage atheism dissolved on contact. And by my senior year of high school, I wound up back in the Catholic Church.

I had bursts of real religious enthusiasm, as teenagers often do. But that larger culture enfolded me again, the one that told me to take things lightly. I explained to people that this was just my chosen form of teenage rebellion. I had obviously been raised in a way that seemed calibrated to make me an ex-Catholic, and I was just subverting expectations. Keeping life on its toes. That is, over time, I was anxious to assure others that nothing about me was so changed that it had to be taken seriously.

———

You say your father prayed five decades of the Rosary with the family each day. At night, your four sisters would file into one bedroom. You and your brother would go in to sleep in the same room with your parents. Your father would climb into bed and pray five decades of the Rosary again with your mother. Years later, in the old folks' home, when nurses and orderlies offended his sense of modesty, he would rage and struggle in his dementia. But these angels attending him learned to just shout the beginning of a prayer. Instantly, the rage subsided, as he started his stiff, ceremonious sign of the cross and joined them in prayer. For you and the usual audiences for the story, the image is funny. For me, it has become something else. In a world where everything is plastic, everything is unserious, this adamantine stubbornness feels like a shelter.

He should have been a priest, you said. And your brother became just that. You remain heathen. Even with all the aid of cruel, holy Ireland and a father willing to drill you in *The Penny Catechism*, which discloses to you the purpose of life and the mysteries of religion in precisely 740 English sentences: Who made you? God made me.

———

In college, the Rising came back to me as well, in history classes where I was advantaged by childhood familiarity with the rebels' names, their views, and their deeds. The hardline revisionists had the courage to take them seriously, alternately detesting and pitying their subjects. Each of the seven men who had signed the Easter Proclamation could be reexecuted in a few words. Tom Clarke: addled by long imprisonment. Joseph Mary Plunkett: dying of tuberculosis, therefore indifferent to life. Seán Mac Diarmada: second-rate radical. Thomas MacDonagh: failed poet, wrote himself into history instead. Éamonn Ceannt: Galway crawthumper. James Connolly, a well-meaning but deluded socialist, who stupidly got himself killed with Patrick Pearse, a boy-crazy creep, the reason Irish people must learn the blasted Irish language in school.

But as time went on, with little distance from the Troubles, with the Celtic Tiger in full swing, the rebels' views became somehow muted and less threatening, and before long no one even offered them the dignity of hating them. Instead of being celebrated or reviled, the rebels were given back to me as trivia and kitsch. They became decorations, men who hung on the wallpaper of O'Connor's Public House, my local. Their great deeds and the songs I knew from childhood extolling them were an ironical source of identity. Their aspirations were not detestable, exactly, but made for good comedy when held against the reality of Ireland today, and when held against me.

Connolly had died convinced that the causes of Ireland and labor were intertwined, but modern and free Ireland was lately hailed as a capitalist miracle. Pearse had believed that Ireland could win a place among sovereign and free nations by reclaiming the creative energy still existing in its Irish-speaking culture, but the great power in Irish culture is English and American media, and the nation's lifeblood is found in the creative way America's tech giants wring continental profits through Irish tax loopholes. Aspiration after aspiration had proven idealistic and naïve, so we hung the idealists' faces on the walls as decoration and made them watch Irish America's version of Erin Go Puke every Paddy's Day. Having them around was like an inside joke about how irrelevant they were.

Your generation makes a different kind of joke about the Rising. I've seen it when you're in St. Sylvester's GAA club. Maybe a man with a Kerry accent cheers a local singer for his rebel song and his Sinn Fein politics. You put on your thickest Dublin accent, asking, "And where were youse when we was doing all the fighting?" As if you yourself, as a Dub, inherit the reputation of having fought in the Rising, and all these culchies inherit the guilt of having sat out Ireland's great hour. When you joke like this, the humor is a backward way of paying tribute to the real thing. The self-deprecation inherent in it is like an act of humility, even gratitude.

What I mean by the Rising becoming kitsch for me is that in my generation, our joke would be to say anything is serious at all. The idea that events and ideals have real meaning, that something outside ourselves deserves our loyalty, is what's ridiculed. We were so conditioned to think of things like honor and shame as delusions. *Ha ha, just imagine dying for a political idea, and what an idiot you'd have to be to do that.* We think this aloofness makes us look unflappable, that it even grants us a certain austere dignity. But it really just makes us satisfied with remaining shallow. We call the higher ideals a form of narrowness, and shrink away from them. Keep an open mind, play the options in front of you. Be smart. Aloof is the safe bet.

But aloofness misleads us. This ironic distance is insufficient when we are really tested. I notice that Sir Roger Casement is now one of the few leaders of the Rising whom Ireland can praise without equivocation. Born in Ireland, he went into imperial service. He became something like the first modern human rights activist, after documenting the abuses of Belgium in the Congo. Gradually he embraced the Irish national cause. Caught off the coast of Kerry trying to deliver weapons from Germany ahead of the Rising, he was tried for treason. Britain exposed his "black diaries," which detailed his sexual preoccupation with young men. And now, I read many articles about how he foreshadowed this more inclusive Ireland. In a recent biography, the author tried to cast him as fully modern in his sensibilities. And at some times in his life, he did take the modern view of things, including religion. He wrote to a friend, "There can be no heaven if we don't find it and make it here and I won't barter this sphere of duty for a hundred spheres and praying wheels elsewhere." And yet that sense of duty eventually carried him beyond what was safe and modern.

In his prison cell, awaiting certain death, he decided he would convert to Catholicism. The archbishop demanded that he recant his Irish nationalism. He refused. But the priests attending him said that he died "with all the faith and piety of an Irish peasant woman."

He wrote a letter explaining himself.

Ireland alone went forth to assail evil, as David Goliath, unarmed, save with a pebble, and she has slain, I pray to God, the power and boast and pride of Empire. That is the achievement of the boys of 1916, and on it the living shall build a sterner purpose, and bring it to a greater end. If I die tomorrow bury me in Ireland, and I shall die in the Catholic Faith, for I accept it fully now. It tells me what my heart sought long in vain—in Protestant coldness I could not find it—but I saw it in the faces of the Irish. Now I know what it was I loved in them— the chivalry of Christ speaking through human eyes—it is from that source the lovable things come, for Christ was the first Knight. And now my beloved ones goodbye—this is my last letter from the condemned cell. I write it always with hope—hope that God will be with me to the end and that all my faults and failures and errors will be blotted out of the Divine Knight—the Divine Nationalist.

These Irish men and women of the Rising and the struggle against England in the years afterward were modern people, which is to say that they were people who could be easily labeled and analyzed by professional historians and our intellectual caste. Their social position could be vivisected: they were a typical revolutionary generation, a rising class of educated people who would be excluded from normal positions of power absent a major shake-up. Their writings and thoughts can be easily tagged—Victorian Gaels, nineteenth-century nationalists, progressive educationists— and then filed away. And yet these people of a century ago had done something that was never supposed to happen. They asserted the rights of the Irish in arms, and won the creation of an Irish state. They had done something that modern people should no longer be able to do in a world of trench warfare, gas attacks, and mass-mechanized death. They became legends. They lived on this edge of life, where aloofness was burned away until some greater conviction emerged.

In quieter moments you have said that you wished you could believe, you just don't. And I know nothing I write or say can change that. Just as the archbishop could not make Roger Casement repent of Ireland's cause. You insist that before the Tiger, Ireland was a dark place. Who, looking at it honestly, can fail to see its faults? Some of its peculiar defects did leave a residue here in America. It could be coldly intellectual. It could become the vindictive enforcer of a Victorian morality that made no sense in Ireland. Even now I find the speed at which Irish Rosary sodalities move through their prayers totally alien and alienating. Worst of all, it abetted child abuse and hid this crime through moral cronyism, elaborately disguised as a fear of scandal.

But the idea that there is nothing for Ireland to do with fifteen centuries of Christianity but celebrate its destruction with dry sherry seems uncreative somehow. If a man like Casement could see something in it, surely there is something you might. The idea that there is nothing "useful" in the Rising for modern Ireland also seems like blindness. There is another Kavanagh poem about Irish religion that haunts me. Often titled "Pilgrims," it found no publisher in his life. It recounts the way Irish people went to a holy well, seeking life, knowledge, and vision, but all related to the immediate necessities of life. "Life that for a farmer is land enough to keep two horses," or "Knowledge that is in knowing what fair to sell the cattle in." But these very practical petitions are answered with something greater.

> I saw them kneeling, climbing and
> prostrate—
> It was love, love, love they found:
> Love that is Christ green walking from
> the summer headlands
> To His scarecrow cross in the turnip-
> ground.

When I was a young man, I was not pushed anywhere near the edge. Unlike Casement, I had nothing like the pride and boast of Empire to confront in life. I had no needs so earthy as those in Kavanagh's poem. But I did choose to confront you. I needed to send you my petitions.

On a Saturday afternoon, I went to the library of my college and ended a decade of silent treatment, of having ignored your letters. I wrote you a long one, trying to condense my teenage years into a dozen or so pages. I was proud to give my report: I'm at a good school. I had learned to fend for myself as my grandmother aged. I could cook. I still watched after my mother. I had one serious girlfriend when I was in high school, and another serious girlfriend now that I was in college. After some journeying, I had come back to Catholicism. At the same time, I tried to demonstrate to you that I was arch, witty, and smart. I was no sucker, or raving lunatic. I wasn't sentimental or self-deluded. All in all, I was a young man to be reckoned with.

I would cringe to reread it now. All the above amounted to a series of not so subtle digs about how different I was from you. *This is who I am*, I seemed to say—and the heavy implication was that you had nothing to do with it. And you ought to get to know me; maybe I'm worth knowing.

But was I worth knowing? I doubt it. Not only was I painfully insecure, I was shallow. Someone who approaches life like a curator will exchange his faith for merely believing in belief. He'll substitute taste where conviction belongs. I was content to slide down the surface of things.

Still, you treated this little gesture as if it could be the basis for going forward. It wasn't long afterward that you and I arranged to meet up in New York. You would bring your wife and your other children, my half siblings whom I'd only met in pictures you sent me. I'd bring that girlfriend, the woman who is now my very pregnant wife.

And soon enough I would find out just how deluded and full of myself I really was.

Your son,
Michael

IV

Marooned by History

O you are not lying in the wet clay,
For it is a harvest evening now and we
Are piling up the ricks against the moonlight
And you smile up at us—eternally.

—*Patrick Kavanagh, "In Memory of My Mother"*

Dear Father,

In the long letter I wrote to you in college, the one where I tried to tell you who I was, I talked about my grandmother dying and its effect on our lives. When I was a child, she had looked after me until Mom came home from work. But in my teenage years, the roles reversed. As I got acne, she got Alzheimer's. And it was my job to keep an eye on her, to make a simple dinner, to be ready to call for help if we needed it. This affliction caused her to misplace herself in the timeline of her own life. At first it was harmless stuff. Instead of saying Clinton was president she might refer to President Reagan, or Nixon. But the sweetness of her spirit began to dim, and a rarer, tougher side came out. It was as if her personality were migrating backward in time, moving from the green hedges, lace curtains, and safety she had attained in the suburbs, and heading back to the childhood streets of New York City. We called it her "Brooklyn chin," when she would push her jaw forward in preparation for battle.

Actually, we preferred her anger to the flashes of despondency and depression. Sometimes Mom and I ignored her little mental mistakes, to save her the embarrassment of correction. Sometimes, in frustration, we pushed back a little, both of us convinced that in certain moments she was "giving in" to this sickness. As if she might, with a moment's pause and sufficient will, renavigate the synapses in her mind, and find a way to be fully present with us.

We wondered at this darker side coming out of

her at the time. But the tortures of her shifting perspective are more obvious to me now than they were then. I can remember her sitting at the table, looking at the newspaper. She mentioned someone's name, a long-deceased relative's, and I could see in that moment that she was living within herself as a younger woman, one with a living husband and young children, seated proudly at her mahogany dining-room set, in the little white home in Bloomfield that she worked so hard to keep neat. In that brief instant she's just enjoying a moment of rest between tidying the kitchen and the living room.

But then she looked up, and instead of her husband, there was I, her teenaged grandson. The mahogany table was still there, beneath her elbows. But the light striking across it and making its surface glow with orange blaze was from the window in her daughter's condo. And in that moment all the losses of her life were reinflicted on her. Her sisters, her husband, her youth, her home, and the sure feeling of a grip of herself. All gone. And the loneliness in that loss staggers me. And now I realize our own frustration at her condition was the effect of her Alzheimer's on us. This disease of the mind also misplaced us in time and history. The moments of anger and bewilderment my mother and I experienced then were the grief and bereavement of the future visiting us in our present. She died on the same day as Princess Diana.

Manhattan was thick with dark blue Yankees caps on the Saturday night that you came, in response to my letter, to meet me again. It was Game 6 of the 2003 World Series against the Florida Marlins. If the Yankees lost, it was over. The city was heavy with a primal, almost manic energy.

You and I were the established diplomats at this meeting. We were the ones who had memories of each other. Everyone else would have to be introduced properly. Your wife and my half siblings to me, and the woman I would marry one day to you. Over dinner you made jokes about how the Irish people were taking advantage of the Celtic Tiger, flying to New York for the very favorable exchange rates. You yourselves were already Christmas shopping that October day. Nothing to declare at the airport, of course. The Irish were now allowed to be flush with cash, but had to keep up the reputation as tax cheats and smugglers.

After dinner, my sisters and your wife departed, and some of my other friends met us out for drinks. They were curious to meet you. The Yankees took Pettitte out of the game and put in Mariano Rivera. Josh Beckett was still pitching into the late innings. I explained to you the mechanics of hits, outs, and strikeouts. And why my friends, all Mets fans, were giggling at the sorry fate of our crosstown rivals. The Yankees' best hitters up in the bottom of the ninth. Bernie Williams, Hideki Matsui, and Jorge Posada. Flyout. Flyout. Groundout. It was over. The citywide fever broke and a spirit of dejection settled on Manhattan. My friends and I clinked glasses. You laughed at this and won them all over.

At the end of the night, you walked my girlfriend and me to the platform in Grand Central. You hugged me and we said our good-byes before I boarded, and the last train of the night pulled me away from you. In a few hours, you'd be over the Atlantic, flying away from me. I felt like it had been a good meeting. The first time we had met without the mediation, or the subsequent fury, of my mother. Maybe this is how we could proceed, as two men. This was my answer to all your charmed visits: At the end of it, I intended you to feel like you had missed out. But even though everything had gone according to my plan, I felt the glow of my victory over you dissipating.

As the train made its way back to my mother's house in the suburbs, my girlfriend told me how she and my siblings studied the two of us as we sat next to each other. You and I each took turns running the table with storytelling. They had been comparing notes through the night, totaling up the expressions and gestures that we shared. They began tallying all these things I had inherited from you—the smirks, and shrugs, a boyish gleam—even though I could not have learned them by imitation. My friends saw the same thing, she said. Everyone could see it, she said. Everyone except me. It began to dawn on me that our relationship wasn't a series of events, but an unalterable and primordial fact. The events were just the record of how we coped with this truth.

My girlfriend and I arrived home at nearly four in the morning and changed for bed. I was trying to change the subject, but she kept talking about you. I lay down and she put her hand on my chest and asked me how I was doing. I said I had realized on that train platform that even though I saw you only a few days or hours at a time in between years of separation, that I could pick you out of a room of a thousand men who were cloned to look like you. And instantly, I was that boy again, standing on Farrandale Avenue. I broke down and bawled my eyes out until sunlight. You leave; I cry. Again.

There was no ironic distance, no getting away from this sorrow. I simply accepted it, in full. I was not fatherless; I had missed you. Not "missed" in the sense of having spent my time pining for your company or in mourning your absence. I didn't pine that way. I had not been an emotional wreck. I had simply missed you, the way one discovers having missed an entire way of life when it is too late.

The facts, only now dawning on me, remained: I had got on with my life in America. You had got on with yours in Ireland. I had passed almost every night from boyhood until that moment without you. I had a father, and I had missed knowing him. That was my story. All the times I had let your letters come to me and returned nothing to you but my callow silence came back to me as reasons to grieve.

Still, there was hope. Something between us changed that day. The cards you sent me for my birthday and Christmas from then on would come alive, with questions about the real details of my life, which for a night you had witnessed. The stories you relayed about my sisters and brother came to me and I could attach them to faces, voices, and personalities I had met. We could build from this, I thought.

Five years after the train station, the woman I love was handmaking thick, stamped, and luxurious invitations for our wedding when she decided to broach the sensitive subject. How would everyone feel if you, your wife, and my siblings came to the wedding? If we did invite you all, where could you be seated to avoid any chance of confrontation with my mother or her brothers? Hadn't they vowed to avenge my mother's honor if they met you again?

At first I dismissed it, but I wondered, Should I go on missing you?

After debating the finer points of seating etiquette, I thought, Let's send them. Let's make a point to show it isn't some empty courtesy. We'll send one invitation for each of them individually. We want them all here and we'll deal with the fallout.

A week later. My phone rang, and you thanked us. So nice of us, you said. Your wife and daughters could not believe that we had ourselves made these complex invitations with maps and gold print. "But Michael," you said, "it wouldn't be right."

"What?"

"It wouldn't be fair to your mother."

"I'm not putting you at the head table. You'll be fine. I promise. My uncles—"

"I can't just show up as your father. After twenty-seven years not there," you said.

We had thought it all through, I protested. But what could I do? Argue you out of feeling ashamed? As a boy I had disclaimed you as father. Now that I was a man, you felt unworthy to stand so close and claim me as your son. Though, you assured me, the invitations were beautiful. And, well, you all appreciated the gesture. You'd visit afterward sometime.

After the wedding, my mother's state continued to worsen. I have often wondered what my flight from home contributed to it. Maybe seeing me settled, she felt like she didn't have to worry so much. She was diagnosed one by one with all the mysterious ailments that strike the lonely and the disconnected: depression, rheumatoid arthritis, and fibromyalgia. And her complaints about them now strike me as mild.

Those mystery ailments had driven her from her job at IBM. She applied for disability, and then did contracting work as a digital assistant to make ends meet. Unknown to me, she also borrowed against the house during the boom and refinanced her debts. The long boom that had underwritten so much stupid optimism in the 1990s was over.

At the time I was torn between the home I was

building with my wife and the home that built me. Mom sent me texts constantly, angling for me to run errands. Could I do "a run" to pick up a takeout dinner she ordered, or to get cigarettes for her? I so often resented these tasks and rolled my eyes. She should have the confidence and where-withal to do them on her own. She shouldn't give in, I thought.

What had happened to my mother? Where was this fiery woman who had backpacked around Europe? The woman with the confidence to wear Cartier and Chanel while picking up her son from play school? Who taught herself to speak Irish from a handful of textbooks and audiocassettes, who wanted to emigrate back across the Atlantic Ocean, who in her love for and rage at you promised she would bomb Ireland if there was one other scoundrel like you in it.

Here she was in middle age, dependent on her son. Ashamed to take his money to fix the heat but too needful to refuse it. She was becoming mysteriously childlike at times. She asked me to do all these errands because they also created a reason for me to come home and spend a little more time with her.

She was frozen in self-doubt. The condo she had bought to put me in a decent school district had shot up to an enormous value during the boom and we had urged her to sell it at the top. She and her mother had bought it in 1994 at a price of $180,000. At the time, the mortgage note was for less than half that price. By 2006, condos like hers were appraising for more than $400,000. We told her to get out of this and downsize. But she couldn't bring herself to do it.

I'd stop over on the way home from work. I remember the octagonal white serviette that I would bring from the kitchen to her bedroom. The items I arranged on it for her were the intersection of bad habits and the worst diet advice that experts ever offered. A giant pink mug full of orange juice, ostensibly for the vitamin C. Next to that another mug of coffee, made with French Vanilla Coffee-mate and three blue packets of sweetener. Next to that a grapefruit. And finally something like rice cakes. Or a "low-fat" frozen bagel, with low-fat cream cheese. Or just some whole wheat toast, supposedly good for the heart. Finally, her pack of Virginia Slims Ultra Lights. I had given up on convincing her to quit smoking. I gently teased and hassled her about the coffee, which I found tedious to prepare, instead.

I remember a night, in the days before Christmas, when I watched her walk up the stairs to her bedroom. In one heel, plantar fasciitis, which tortured her with sharp pangs. In the other leg, bruises, a dull pain that made her uncertain and unsteady. She barely had the breath to lift her limbs. Her state was enough to overwhelm me with helpless guilt and anger. And yet, this image of her, a lonely and sad wreck, is transfigured now, when I recall it. After all, she pushed through the pain. She endured—stubbornly and patiently—the financial stress, determined not to let me know too much about it. And that ascent up the stairs was the most impressive feat of physical courage I have ever seen with my own eyes. She moved one step ahead of me, slowly, deliberately, cautiously, but *willfully.*

A few days after that climb up the stairs, her best friends came in and surprised her by staying through Christmas. She and they came and sat at my dining-room table for breakfast on Christmas Day, and she smiled at me, happy to see me settled in a home and with a good wife. By her lights, I had turned out well. She explained that she wanted eight grandchildren and soon. We all laughed that she should have had more kids if she wanted that.

Her friends went back to London after New Year's Day. Two days later, while I worked, she and

I sent each other messages about a new Winnie the Pooh movie coming out. She had decorated my childhood room with these characters, and they always made me think of her. "We should see it together," she wrote back. A few hours later, I got a call that she was being rushed to the hospital. I rushed there, to find her already dead.

After I called her brother and best friend, I called you. "Do you need me to come over," you asked, "to stand by you?" I didn't think so, no. We hung up and I tried to turn to funeral preparations.

My grief did not wait until I had finished making all the phone calls and arrangements. My wife and I retreated to her parents' home across town. They tried to console me, but their presence only emphasized the difference between families like theirs, intact and together, and my own. Everyone from my wife's childhood home could gather in an hour's time on my account. My closest blood relation was three thousand miles away, and had to ask whether he should come.

Some people feel a guilty sense of liberation when their parents die. They feel they finally have escaped a shadow. I felt nothing like that. In the face of my mother's suffering and death, I saw my whole world, my whole way of being, as counterfeit. The myth of the darkened past giving way to light was obviously wrong. In the past was my mother as she had been—strong, independent, and full of fight. In the future there was no way to make up to her for all the eyerolls and the guilt I inflicted on her when all she wanted was the company of her son.

Even the version of religious faith I had re-adopted suddenly seemed like a fake. I wanted the sweet consolations and mercies it offered. I had wanted meaning *for myself*, and I wanted salvation *for myself*. I had disguised the culture's idea of freedom from judgment under the vestments of Christian forgiveness to make it more convincing.

Just fifteen months earlier, at my wedding rehearsal, my mother had responded with perfect meekness to the priest who invited any penitents in my wedding party to confession. Having been away for decades, she asked for some encouragement from me, and I gave her some. I loudly claimed to believe in this faith, but it was she, who made no such boasts, who suffered like a saint. I know that canonizing one's mammy is another Irish cliché. So be it.

I felt grief, and soon I would feel fury too. A perfect zealous hatred burned through me as I went through her papers, frantically searching for some guidance on her will or on any life insurance policy. I discovered that in the last weeks of her life she was approved for yet another refinance of her home loan, made in line with the terms of a new federal bailout program. The terms should have been criminal. The monthly payment would eat up more than two thirds of her Social Security disability check. And the payments would stretch on for forty years longer. Under the guise of helping her and stabilizing the economy, someone collected a fee when the very sick middle-aged woman on the other side of the table from him signed on the dotted line. This agreement would make her home a debtor's prison and keep her on subsistence, while she paid off nearly three quarters of a million dollars of debt for the rest of her life. The Irish in history killed or emigrated to escape tenancy terms less onerous than this. She died before the first payment was due. But here I was, looking at a contract that, in an age that had any sense of duty beyond self-enrichment, would have inspired widespread rancor and war upon the wicked.

My mother was a child of her age. She believed that people would accept her decisions. And for the rest of her life, she paid dearly for it. Despite all the happy talk in America about an enlightened age accommodating all kinds of families, she still experienced shame on my account. She lost a job over being an unmarried mother. As the unmarried daughter in an Irish American family, the primary responsibility of watching over and then taking care of her aged parents was left to her. Men paid her less attention than she deserved. After all, she was carrying baggage.

Now I see, she was carrying a cross.

I was furious too at the ambivalence of our culture in the face of her death. This myth of liberation was like a solvent that had slowly and inexorably dissolved any sense of obligation in life. It dissolved the bonds that held together past, present, and future. It dissolved the social bonds that hold together a community, and that make up a home. And, here at the end of the process, I was alone. An atom that becomes separated from a larger chemical structure is called a free radical.

And that is how I felt, supercharged with this urgent longing to reconnect to something larger.

A healthy culture provides all the proper ceremony for death; it gives rituals that allow people to grieve as individuals, and families. But in an age of self-creation, of a curated life, lived in row houses where people hardly know their neighbors, the bereaved are confronted with an endless series of menus and options. All provided at exorbitant cost.

The modern Church too was useless. I felt nothing but sorrow and inadequacy in the face of her death. I felt like, in penance, we should be made to pray for my mother, to ask forgiveness for the wrongs and slights we inflicted or allowed. But without me frantically managing the Church myself, it would have given us its new ceremony, everyone at the altar dressed in white, like at a hospital, anesthetizing us with a feeling of unearned peace. It would have provided a stranger at the lectern, giving banalities about a "better place" that we all would have pretended to find consoling. A healthy culture lets you know what is right and proper, so that only when the great work is done, you find a peace worth having. Instead, I asked for a proper requiem, with a priest dressed in black, music that expressed hope but in the only way hope can make sense, calling out from within a present shadowed by sorrow, grief, guilt, and shame.

Everyone from my childhood home was now dead. I was at the end of history, yes, marooned there. I had no siblings who could give me the consolation that comes through retold memories that are shared only in the intimacy of a family home. I had no grieving widower father who needed support more than I did. As yet, I had no children in whom I could find a mission, or at least a living sign of that hope.

Hours into this ugly, furious scramble to find the resources—financial, spiritual—to bury my mother, I called you again. I called you feeling enraged at you too. Yes, your relationship with my mother was a fraught wreck, or, at least, my existence made it one. But could you not see that it didn't matter what I claimed to need, or what I felt? This woman had raised your son. I steadied my voice, the way my mother tried to when she wanted her feelings cast aside in a decision: "I don't need you to come," I said. "You should come for *yourself.*"

I knew with awful clarity that night: This grief would follow me for years. I still had this guilty feeling that somehow my existence ruined her life. Without me, she could have moved back to London, where she was happy. Without me, she could have found a husband. And now, every happiness in my own life would be shadowed by her absence.

I told my wife that when I was young and excited about my favorite basketball players, I would run up the stairs almost every commercial break or time-out and interrupt whatever my mother was doing to report on their disappointments or exult in their triumphs. My mother tolerated these intrusions into her life with perfect patience and equanimity. Of course she did. One day, I would have my own disappointments and triumphs to rush to her. This was all a mock rehearsal for the real satisfactions of life ahead.

And how I wish she was here for this one. We expect our daughter to arrive any day now. And though I am very, very happy to get on with this next phase of life, I wish I could share it with my mother. She had been asking for this, longing for this day, and bothering us to bring it about in the last days of her life, with some of her last breath. She will never meet one of her own grandchildren. There's no shrinking from that fact. Or from the way this coming triumph in my life is ringed with bittersweetness and sorrow.

From a very young age, I vowed that if I had

children I would not raise them in a broken home like mine. But my fear is that, no matter how well I keep one together, I don't know how to repair the brokenness that surrounds the home, this malady that afflicts us all, that dissolves all connection between past, present, and future. This thing that makes our grandparents into strangers to us, that leaves us disconnected from one another, ill equipped to meet these moments in life, when real injustice, real sorrow, and real grief visit us.

Your son,
Michael

V

Rebel Songs As Lullabies

The great Gaels of Ireland
Are the men that God made mad,
For all their wars are merry,
And all their songs are sad.

—*G. K. Chesterton,*
"The Ballad of the White Horse"

Dear Father,

You visited again, not long after Mom died. I had the unique privilege in life of inviting my father into my own home before I'd ever been in his. We went to lunch in town and you asked me something I hadn't anticipated: "Do you have anything you want to say to me, Michael?"

It was bold of you to ask. We hadn't spent even three months in each other's presence in the past twenty-nine years of my life.

You repeated the question a few times, because instead of answering I was probing for the reason you asked. Something to say in light of my mother's death? Or, as a man? We normally keep things light. Did you want me to lay into you? Were we finally going to have it out? Would I finally put the guilt on your head? Would I let out my secret hurts?

I don't think of you as very calculating, but there was something artful about the way you asked. You said it as though it would be perfectly normal if I did, and that it would be perfectly fitting for you to hear it. There was no pressure on me either. That we spoke about it in a restaurant kept the threat of bursting into anger or tears safely at a distance.

Rather than answer, I gave you a canned description of my childhood without you. You would come and visit, maybe once every two years or so. You would stay for a few weeks. You would dote on me and then you would have to leave. I would be disconsolate for a week or so thereafter, and my mother resented you for it. She thought you were somehow enjoying the pride of fatherhood, and leaving her with the rest. You already knew this story of our nonrelationship, one my mother had told you over and over again.

On that day, I couldn't confront your question honestly. "Do you have anything you want to say to me?" Aside from those days immediately after you left, I said, the experience of your absence was just that: an absence. Like the big scabs on my knees from a crash on my bike, it was something I picked at for a few days until it disappeared. And then I went out and played.

I was trying to soothe you. To relieve you of guilt.

I had also grown up and married, and in the school of life had made a study myself, I told you. I knew that only a few decisions separated us. If things had gone just slightly differently, I could someday be sitting as you were that day, inviting my estranged son to have it out with me. I wrapped it all up by saying that, by the standards of the world, I was happy and successful. I was not in jail. I had a job, lived in a nice town, and had a beautiful wife. And that made everything easier for both of us, didn't it? As if to underline the point, I ordered an espresso, and at the end of the meal, I offered to pay.

Afterward, I congratulated myself on my maturity. I felt I had paved a way forward for us. We had a complex history, sure. But we could be men about it. There's no wrecked life that can be blamed on you. There's nothing I lack that can be held against you.

How evasive! How beside the point! I had recast our estrangement as just the unfortunate mistake you made in conceiving me. Too bad about your firstborn son being three thousand miles away and knowing nothing about you. I had reframed your fatherhood as merely one among many conveniences I happened to miss in a life otherwise defined by middle-class success and material acquisition. I don't know how you view our history, but please forgive me for suggesting this was mine. Just as one day it dawned on me that I had missed you, I realize now: You had missed me.

It's as if this language of getting ahead and technocratic manipulation becomes the default mode of thinking around us, and we adapt ourselves to it when we don't know what to say. I'm discovering now how much parenting advice and guidance is packaged this way, how it recasts fathers not merely as providers, but as social engineers, as "wonks." Read to your child, because children who read with their parents on average make a million dollars more over life. Eat dinner with your child, because a child who eats at a family table becomes more sociable and in the long run will marry better and get more promotions. Cuddle with a child; cuddled children get better mortgage rates as adults. As if parenthoods could be judged by the grades we got in school, or the salaries we achieved.

When my daughter makes eye contact with me, all of this talk is revealed as nonsense. As totally beside the point. This advice presumes love is the base input, an animal instinct that is transmuted by a civilizing process into the thing that matters—wealth, advantage, and status. I know now, viscerally, what nonsense this is, what a profanation it is.

It's been a few weeks since we brought our daughter home from the hospital. We are, like all new parents, sleep deprived and discombobulated. I think it's only just dawning on us what this responsibility entails for us moment to moment. In some ways, we are living in a constant repeat of the first night she came to us. After a long labor, my wife needed more attention from the doctors, so my daughter and I were put into a dark room by ourselves, for nearly an hour. I stripped off my shirt, pressed her next to me, and sang over and over again the same songs: "The West's Awake," "The Foggy Dew," "The Wind That Shakes the Barley," even "The Patriot Game," which I try to sing in that lullaby way Liam Clancy did.

I do the same thing over and over now when she cries and resists the comforts of sleep. I know it sounds crazy. She screams bloody murder, and I sing about blood and murder. This experience, of immersing her and myself in these songs and in this history, has given me a new way of seeing not just our relationship, but the world.

The New York Times has started running articles about the centennials being commemorated in Dublin. One of them said recently that the men of the Rising claimed to act on the authority of "the dead generations, who could not demur." In those last four words is a view of Irish history—of everything, really—that these songs no longer permit me. I recognize in those words "the men of letters" in your generation, and a younger version of myself, the one who thought he had put away all delusions. The dead are just silent. What else could they be?

And what is a nation? In this way of thinking, a nation is at best a problematic, if still useful, administrative unit. That is, it's merely the arena in which technocrats and wonks do their work of making improvements on society. And now our men of letters cannot develop a political or moral thought without searching out a social science abstract from which to loot it. Most of the time, I find they don't read the studies. Why bother? The authors of the studies know what the wonks desire to say, and design studies to give their words the look of authority. It's a perpetual-motion machine.

And like a machine, it generates only the illusion of a working intelligence inside it.

From where I sit, the Easter Rising and its popularity has been misunderstood by the great and the good from the moment it began. It is almost as if the Rising happened behind a veil that excluded respectable opinion: In today's Irish papers the Rising is denounced as a senseless, theocratic plot. In the exact same papers in 1916 it was denounced as senseless communist agitation. Within a week of the events, the Rising became known on Irish streets and in British government offices as the "Sinn Fein Rebellion," even though Sinn Fein had almost nothing to do with it. The Rising was misidentified by the authorities and misunderstood by the approved commentators even before its leaders were executed.

What I think bothers official Ireland most about the Rising is that its leaders were so thoroughly vindicated, in ways that are impossible to justify through the accepted terms of social science and technocracy. In military terms the Rising failed, as its leaders anticipated. But they also knew that Ireland would be so inflamed by their deeds that she would one day seize independence. They wanted to redeem the city of Dublin from its complicity in colonial rule, and Dublin streets and buildings found their place in a people's ballads. They predicted that their names would be entered into the long and glorious roll of Irish rebels; and they are, all of them, at the head. Ever since, historians have been trying to catch up to them, trying to explain how everything went wrong, and yet exactly according to plan. How was it that a band of radical poets and language activists won a fight that they lost, a fight that Ireland had lost, one way or another, for centuries every time it was tried? They still cannot see it.

———

Even before they fired a shot, it became clear to those leading the Easter Rising that their revolutionary plot was botched. On the preceding Good Friday, Sir Roger Casement was captured off the coast of Kerry by British forces while trying to deliver twenty thousand German guns to Irish rebels. His capture alerted the head of the Irish Volunteers, Eoin MacNeill, to the plot unfolding among his men. The shock was horrible. The paramilitary he supposedly commanded was about to be hijacked by a tiny faction hell-bent on bloody rebellion. Some of the troops themselves didn't know their planned "drills" that Easter Sunday would end in violence.

MacNeill was not opposed to a violent rebellion in theory, but he took Casement's capture as evidence that this rebellion would fail and so be immoral. He issued a countermanding order in the Sunday newspapers, informing all units of the Volunteers that drills and movements had been canceled that day. He also ordered Michael Joseph O'Rahilly to drive all over the country to give word that the Rising was off.

In the heart of this moment, a father looks at his daughter, and is unmanned. Nora Connolly, then eighteen, went to see her father, James, the socialist commander of the Irish Citizen Army. "I said to him, 'Daddy we're not going to fight?' He turned to me and two big tears rolled down his cheeks. He says, 'If we don't fight, Nora, we can only pray for an earthquake to come and swallow us and our shame.'"

Funny thing about Connolly: Although he professed materialism, he believed that on a single moment of action he and his fellows would be judged. He was a socialist, but he had nothing of the wonk about him.

The military council of the Irish Republican Brotherhood settled on launching the Rising, even if just in Dublin, the next day. They had good reason to go ahead. When word got out about a canceled rebellion, the Volunteers would be suppressed. They had some flimsier reasons, like the hope that if they could hold out long enough, the whole country would be inspired to follow. But the decisive factor was that after all they had said and done, their sense of honor forbade them to go home. The cause of an independent Ireland was too dear and too fragile. It might be lost if they did not act in that hour.

A year before, Pearse had given the oration at the graveside of O'Donovan Rossa, the militant Irish nationalist who, decades earlier, had been part of the Fenian rebellions, a series of doomed attempts in the 1960s to win an Irish Republic through a campaign of violence in Ireland, England, and even the Americas. Before his death, Rossa spent years rotting in an English prison. Pearse's panegyric connected the last several Irish rebellions together into an apostolic succession. And he placed his generation next in line after the Fenians:

> Life springs from death; and from the graves of patriot men and women spring living nations. The Defenders of this Realm have worked well in secret and in the open. They think that they have pacified Ireland. They think that they have purchased half of us and intimidated the other half. They think that they have foreseen everything, think that they have provided against everything; but the fools, the fools, the fools!—they have left us our Fenian dead, and while Ireland holds these graves, Ireland unfree shall never be at peace.

Pearse's speech was heard far beyond the graveside. Men and boys recited it in train stations and alongside the pitch at hurling matches.

Late on Easter Sunday, the O'Rahilly, as he was known, arrived at Liberty Hall covered in grime to beg Pearse and Connolly to desist. They heard his case but were not convinced. The next morning, when the sound of gunfire began to fill the city, the O'Rahilly presented himself in uniform. "It is madness, but it is glorious madness," he said.

As a piece of military planning, the Rising in Dublin gave plenty of evidence of having been drawn up by a poet. The rebels started digging trenches in St. Stephen's Green on Monday morning, but trenches are of little use when surrounded by tall buildings. The Shelbourne Hotel was used by British marksmen to shoot out the rebels there. Many of the fighting men spent much of the Rising hunkered down in buildings, with no fight to join. Along with the glorious madness, there was the usual sort as well. A gunfight in a hospital ward full of moaning patients and quaking nuns. A British cavalry charge bearing down on commuters. Rebels begging Dublin's poor not to disgrace Ireland's great hour with their looting.

Probably the worst disaster of planning was their failure to seize Dublin Castle, the seat of English rule for seven hundred years. Connolly's Citizen Army made a little charge at it. They killed one man protecting the gate (an Irishman), but ran away under fire. Had they done even cursory snooping beforehand, they would have known that just six men guarded a castle whose capture would have been a grand symbolic victory.

In the midst of the bumbling, there were moments of real daring. During the battle, two men, Michael Malone and Jim Grace, holed up in the bathroom of 25 Northumberland Road. Just these two pinned down a whole column of British reinforcements with sniper fire. Confused by the sounds of echoes and ricochets, the British thought they were being fired at by hundreds of men. A few more Irishmen came into the battle from a position on Mount Street. Finally, the British stormed number 25 and shot Malone. Grace escaped out the window. There were two hundred thirty British casualties to four Irish. You and I, not so long ago, stood on this very street watching people making their way home past number 25, unconscious that they were tromping through the site of Ireland's Thermopylae.

Why was the O'Rahilly inspired to report for duty by the sound of gunfire in Dublin? Why did the Irish come to accept this small revolutionary putsch as representative of their aspirations? The typical Irish attitude of self-deprecation, of gombeen self-abasement, is a dam holding back deep waters. The Rising dynamited that dam. *The New York Times* tells me the dead generations could not demur from the Rising launched in their name. In fact, I now know that the dead generations were clamoring for it.

One of Ireland's younger historians, Fearghal McGarry, examines the testimonies of common people who participated in and witnessed the Rising. Men and women of all classes had been formed by nationalist histories and songs of rebellion. Many of them grew up with pictures of nationalist heroes like Wolfe Tone in their homes. "Thanks to my mother's great fund of Irish songs and ballads, I was familiar with Ireland's struggle for independence long before I could read or write," said one man, one among millions. The Rising resonated with the ancient, near-liturgical repeatings of Irish history. The Gaelic clans that fought the Normans, the confederacy that battled the Tudors, the Fenians who launched themselves at the empire. These were all the antetypes, anticipating a rebellion that would one day succeed. A ballad history of songs and stories taught the Irish to know their deliverers when they came.

One of the obstacles for Irish nationalists was that the status of being a "beaten race" caused the Irish not to take their country all that seriously, at least in public. You could sing the old songs in private, but being a "mad Irishman" was treated as an affectation. And yet, here in this one place were serious-looking Irishmen, and elevated words about Irish history. C. S. Andrews recalled the effect on his teenage imagination of seeing the Volunteers at O'Donovan Rossa's graveside commemoration and in demonstrations in the autumn of 1915:

> For me they were a wonderful sight. I was sure that they were going to set Ireland free and avenge the Croppies of '98, and I was reminded that one of the few successes of the '67 Fenian Rising was at Stepaside and Glencullen where the manoeuvres were tak-

ing place. I lay in a field under the Three Rock Mountain gazing over the beautiful countryside and imagining British battleships steaming into the bay and being blown to bits by guns which, in my imagination, I placed at strategic points around the hills.

———

There was resistance to this romantic view, of course. Yeats's poem "Easter, 1916" is not really about the way the rebels had "changed, changed utterly" the living stream of Irish history, but how the view of the men who had been in the Rising had been changed by the fight. These once-annoying zealots and poets were now martyrs. "What if excess of love bewildered them till they died?" Yeats asked.

An excess of love? I think there is something about human nature, or everyday life, that makes us suspect that whatever is real lacks meaning. And whatever is meaningful is not grounded in reality. We are tempted to think we are simply deluding ourselves, bewildered, and imposing our dreamed-up ideas on matter, which is indifferent. That suspicion may be operating in the background when we lazily dismiss a political idea as mere narrative. It is working behind and through all that stupid baby advice that gives up on describing a parent's love as it is, and instead searches for some social statistic to justify it. It works on us when we put so many layers of ideology between ourselves and the past. As if the one lesson of history is that the past has nothing to teach us. Yeats could imagine a love of Ireland that inspired men to worship her through his stage plays. But to actually die for her seemed to him excessive. A woman Yeats loved understood the Rising better, and rebuked him with her judgment: "Tragic dignity has returned to Ireland."

We are used to conceiving of the nation almost exclusively as an administrative unit. A nation is measured by its GDP, its merit is discovered in how it lands on international rankings for this or that policy deliverable. A nation may have a language, but the priority is to learn the lingua franca of global business. Our idea of doing something for the nation is reduced to something almost exclusively technical. Policy wonks are the acknowledged legislators of our world.

But there is nothing technical about the Rising. I see in the Rising that a nation cannot live its life as a mere administrative district or as a shopping mall; nations have souls. It's a virtue when poetry colonizes our politics, even if today the situation is reversed. The life of a nation is never reducible to mere technocracy, just as the home cannot be, no matter how much we try to make it so. I see that nationality is something you do, even with your body, even with your death. I see that a history of plunder does not oblige those plundered to despair; it obliges them to hope, and to act on that hope.

By the time they surrendered on Friday, Dublin had the look of desolation. The British soldiers were appalled to discover the small number of men who had put up such a fight against them. And they were nonetheless impressed by the military bearing and dignity of the rebels. The Volunteers took pride in themselves, marching in columns, led by their officers, many of whom had given them a kind of valedictory speech at the end. "We have won what we have fought for," Éamonn Ceannt said to his group. "You may not see it now, but you will see it soon." A wonk would never recognize that a losing fight can be a victory in itself. Perhaps only an Irishman can see it. "We were satisfied that all things that were possible had been done. There was nothing to be ashamed of." Yes, in the eyes of many of the onlookers, the Dubliners who spat on them, it was madness. Glorious nonetheless.

———

While marching into the custody of British soldiers, some of the Irish Volunteers saw the body of the O'Rahilly. There on Moore Street, lying in his own blood, was the man who had traveled the country, carrying with him the calculated view, the wonk's view. And yet, he let himself be converted from ambivalence to action. Knowing what was next for him, he found a letter from his own son in his pocket and wrote on the back of it:

> Written after I was shot—Darling Nancy, I was shot leading a rush up Moore Street took refuge in a doorway. While I was there I heard the men pointing out where I was & I made a bolt for the lane I am in now. I got

more [than] one bullet I think. Tons and tons of love dearie to you & to the boys & to Nell & Anna. It was a good fight anyhow.

A beaten race does not produce men like this.

It's almost impossible to describe the effect on me to even read about deeds like this. I cannot imagine the effect on others who saw the Volunteers marching so manfully into the hands of their captors. You can't help but ask yourself, Would I do the same? Perhaps that is a boyish thought, like those of C.S. Andrews.

There is a way of doing things that is, in itself, persuasive. Sometimes just doing them is its own argument. You can look at the Rising and the cultural revival and say that Irish nationalism, like many nationalisms, is an ideological technology for gaining sovereignty. But that seems to me to take things to a level of abstraction that makes them false. Ireland is a nation. We know this because the English treated it like a foreign country despite an act of union. Ireland is a nation because men in uniforms marched and died for it. Ireland will be recognized as a republic because Patrick Pearse and the signatories declared it so, and died to make it so.

All the nationalist ballads that men sung aloud might have made them feel silly in the years before the Rising. But it was these ballads that allowed them to know when tragic dignity returned to Ireland.

A rebel of an earlier generation, Thomas Davis, saw exactly how it would work.

A Ballad History is welcome to childhood, from its rhymes, its high colouring, and its aptness to memory. As we grow into boyhood, the violent passions, the vague hopes, the romantic sorrow of patriot ballads are in tune with our fitful and luxuriant feelings.

In manhood we prize the condensed narrative, the grave firmness, the critical art, and the political sway of ballads. And in old age they are doubly dear; the companions and reminders of our life, the toys and teachers of our children and grandchildren.

These men and women allowed themselves to be refashioned from something outside themselves. They were ambitious men, of course, but they let the words and deeds of the past weigh on them and refashion them. When two men hide in a bathroom and pin down a column of soldiers, when a man joins the glorious madness of a doomed battle to preserve the pride of his nationality, when men march happily into the hands of their captors, and commend the executors, a dying nation rises to life.

Could self-made men do this? Or men who are clever, but think nobility itself a delusion? Could it be done by men who suspected that the world and what we do in it is, at bottom, meaningless?

———

I've only in the last year come to understand the weight of your words to me. I brought my daughter home just two weeks ago; you welcomed me into your home for the first time just last year. My wife and I told ourselves we would go to Ireland and do it like tourists. I had told her about how beautiful the west of the country was. How much Galway and the Aran Islands had impressed themselves on me in my childhood. In some ways, we would retrace my mother's trips around the island. I stood in the harbor where the Irish resistance was beaten in 1602. We toured around the ruins at the Rock of Cashel, where in 1843 three hundred thousand Irish men and women gathered to demand repeal of Ireland's union with Great Britain. In town, with you, we passed by the sites of the Rising.

All of that would have been good enough. But we took you up on the new offer to stay with you part of the time. My half brother vacated his bedroom so that the two of us could pile in. You had always written to me to tell me of my siblings and how they were getting on in life. And you passed on their greetings and best wishes for me. I never knew whether to believe it. But now, for the first time, I saw that on the wall of their childhood home there were pictures of me. My sisters explained to me, around your table, how their friends and teachers often thought they were making something up, with their talk of an American brother. On your refrigerator was a picture of all of us together, on that night the Yankees lost it all in New York. Our first dinner as a family. At night, you'd walk us down the hill, and we'd all tuck into your local haunts. Your friends would greet you, and as if it were the most natural thing in the world, you introduced me. "This is my son Michael," from America. Maybe they'd raise an eyebrow. Or joke about what other secrets you might be keeping. And then, each and every one would say what Irish people so often said to Yanks who arrive in their midst: "Welcome home."

I didn't yet feel like I had any right to Ireland as home. The distance that opened up between us on the hurling pitch has haunted me ever since. But, as I bound around our little home, amidst the anonymous suburbs of New York, with this treasure in my arms, I am singing these songs, about deeds done on the Shannon's waves, or in the green and lovely lanes of Killeshandra, and the distance is starting to close.

And something else is transformed now too. You'd missed my baptism, as you would miss all those events marking my life. But when your granddaughter was born, you got the call within the first hours. You heard her crying. I told you the songs I sang. And you told me that your father, the grandfather I never knew, would appreciate that I sang "The Patriot Game," the one featuring his home county. And soon you'll be here for her baptism, and she'll learn to speak the words "granddad" and "Ireland" in full certainty that these names are real, close, and that they are a source of shelter and love for her.

Your son,
Michael

VI

Father Tongue

A people without a language of its own is
only half a nation. . . . To lose your native
tongue, and learn that of an alien,
is the worst badge of conquest.

—*Thomas Davis*

Dear Father,

In one of my mother's letters to you, she wrote, "If I judged Ireland on the likes of you, I'd see it bombed." And then a few lines later, "Can you get ahold of the following book, *Nuachúrsa Gaeilge na mBráithre Críostaí*? We're surviving on photocopies." Knowing, as you do, the ambivalence about the Irish language in Ireland, that must have been a strange request to get from an American ex-girlfriend. I'm astonished at her daring. A single, working mother, handling IBM's great executives, taking care of her child and her mother, determined to learn this dying language, even if she has to recruit the efforts of a man she'd just as well see bombed.

My mother achieved real competence in Irish, and then gradually lost it. Her exertions were motivated by this unrequited love, her ambitions, and even her politics. After she died, I found all these great propaganda pamphlets from the early 1980s, with titles like "Britain's War Machine in Ireland." All of it aimed at Irish Americans like herself. But it was hard, in the exurbs of New York with a dying mother and a growing son, to keep up the social circles that support a language. And gradually even we stopped using the ornamental bits of it.

And right now the ornamental bits of it are almost all I have. When I've gone through my cycle of rebel songs, I have tried soothing this baby girl by counting in Irish. Or whispering, over and over, *Mo chroi, mo thaisce.* My heart, my treasure.

I came upon something funny in all this reading. Patrick Pearse once wrote a fantasy of what Ireland might be like one century after his time. He envisioned the Ireland of 2005 as a warmer place, because the bogs had been drained. And he envisioned it as a country in which the Irish language was restored totally. Only a few schools still taught it as a second language. With the collapse of the British Empire in the twentieth century— he was right about that!—the English language lost its importance. In his dream, the Irish Parliament in 2005 was debating a bill for making the study of Japanese compulsory in seaport towns in Ireland, owing to its utility as a commercial language.

The story didn't go that way. I wrote to you earlier about the plunder of Ireland. How the English have robbed Ireland not just of its wealth, and of many of its lives, but of its sense of self. After the Famine, the Irish mind awakened to the possibility of losing even the memory of itself. And it responded with a self-conscious attempt at cultural revival.

What most people say is that the Gaelic cultural revival of the late nineteenth and early twentieth centuries produced a lot of good and some great literature in English—Yeats, Joyce, and so on. And the revival of Irish sport under the Gaelic Athletic Association was a crushing success. I know because I can listen live to the broadcast of Mayo and Dublin fighting to a draw in Gaelic football on my smartphone. But we are supposed to conclude that the language revival was doomed, and possibly destructive to have tried. In his book about the history of Irish language, Aidan Doyle concludes, "Anybody who sets himself an impossible task is bound to fail. My contention . . . is that by the time the Gaelic League was founded, it was too late to reverse the language shift. If this is correct there was never a real possibility of Irish becoming a majority language in Ireland again."

So should we all have a laugh at Pearse? Currently there are more than 400 million native English speakers in the world. Some estimates say that nearly one in five people on the planet are studying or speaking English as a second language. In many places, studying English is compulsory. The numbers for Irish are not so encouraging. I remember the day I began contemplating the current estimated number of native Irish speakers: thirty-five thousand.

A little while after I made my vow to learn Irish, my father-in-law took me to Colorado for an event commemorating the World War II company his father was in, the one that cut up through Europe from Anzio and eventually liberated Dachau. At the hotel in the morning, instead of doing a little lesson of Irish on a website I was subscribed to, I was reading *The Irish Times*, with the latest report on how the Gaeltacht, the various regions of Ireland where Irish is still spoken daily, was dying. By 2025 Irish will cease to be a majority language in the Gaeltacht, it said. The latest studies showed that once the percentage of Irish speakers in these areas fell below 67 percent, Irish would become a language of the old; the young would fail to develop freedom of expression in Irish and would instead form their identity and self-conception as English speakers. This is a disaster for the language for obvious reasons. The Gaeltacht is where almost all serious students of the Irish language finally finish acquiring it. The few tens of thousands of native Irish speakers today already struggle to support the compulsory learning of the hundreds of thousands of students of the language in Irish schools. And most of these students will fail to acquire it anyway. Beyond that, the Gaeltacht still has some pull as a physical and spiritual heartland of the nation, the repository of true Irishness.

Contemplating this report, I had some questions. Why the hell was I trying to learn Irish? It takes real effort to learn a language, and often a decent chunk of money too. I got up from the desk and thought about that number. Thirty-five thousand native speakers, and I spent a couple of hundred dollars on kids' books and dictionaries, and a subscription learning website. Thirty-five thousand native speakers, and none of my actual Irish family members is counted among them. Not one of them is even in the half million or so who are categorized, generously, as competent second-language speakers of Irish. Thirty-five thousand. If I go through with this, I am a madman.

I got into a little tour van that was going to take us to the sights for that day, and I sat next to a man named Randy Palmer. He had a big, round Oklahoman accent, and his baritone voice made him sound like a Plains-state version of David Carradine. He was a member of the Kiowa nation and a veteran of the Vietnam War. Because I was thinking about languages, I asked him if he spoke the language of the Kiowa nation. He didn't. He said that a few of the young people were interested

in it. So then and there, I furtively started re-
searching on my phone. There are only twelve
thousand Kiowa living. And a generous estimate
is that there are just a hundred speakers of the
Kiowa language. None of them speak it as a
mother tongue. Like most Native American languages, it had no writing system until long after
most people had abandoned speaking it. The very
first orthography for the language wasn't developed until the 1920s. And talk of attempting a
language revival really only started in the last five
years. I have since been cheered to discover that at
least one children's book has been published in
Kiowa. Instead of thirty-five thousand Irish who
have known the language from their cribs within
Irish-speaking communities, the number is zero
for Kiowa. All Kiowa grow up speaking English
with big Plains-state accents.

That night, Palmer played a CD recording of
the Kiowa Black Leggings Warrior chant for the

157th Battalion's annual military ball. That was the Kiowa language as it exists right now, completely fossilized. And in that form it moved many young men to tears. Here was the tongue of a people, and a nation, disappearing from the face of the earth. And when the party ended late that night, I went back to my bed in the hotel, plugged earphones into my phone, and listened to a live, morning news radio show in Irish.

You see the difference? One is purely ceremonial. The other is fit for radio broadcast and current events.

Pearse was more right to imagine Irish as a living language in this century. It is alive in a way that Kiowa isn't. I sincerely hope one day, if my great-grandchildren have an interest in Native American languages, they can pull up a live internet radio stream in the Kiowa language. Perhaps we can program computers to produce these even if the Kiowa language revival fails among the twelve thousand living Kiowa today. But Irish still survives. And it is this way because of the revivalists. When Pearse and other language activists came to the Irish language it was heading where Kiowa is now.

The truth is that there are more people who are literate in Irish today than two centuries ago, when our best estimates are that twenty thousand Irish speakers had any literacy in their mother tongue, even if over 2 million were fluent speakers of the language. The decline of Irish happened for many reasons. It was the aim of the English government to destroy it. Sir Edmund Spenser observed, "The speech being Irish, the heart must needs be Irish." Even in the sixteenth century, the Irish would use their native language to resist English rule. As the Tudors sent their ministers to rule, they found not just the Gaelic Irish but also the descendants of the Normans refusing to speak in an English language they knew, just to annoy and frustrate the will of their rulers. "Though they could speak English as well as wee, yet Commonly speake Irish among themselves, and were hardly included by our familiar Conversation to speak English with us, yea Common experience shewed and my selfe and others observed the Citizens of Watterford and Corcke having wyves that could speak English as well as wee, bitterly to chyde them when they speake English with us."

During the time of the penal laws, Irish was the language of the most fierce resistance to English rule. The Irish nationalists who spoke in English tended to be reformists, republicans, and modernizers, and spoke of "improvement" with language meant to appease English rulers. But Irish-language poetry teemed with Jacobite fury and dark prophecies about the English being brought low into disgrace as scholars of the Irish language retake their place at the top of society. They were close to right. Eventually the authority of the English did decline. And while I wouldn't say Irish scholars are at the top of society, they at least get positions on TV and radio now, and the occasional column in *The Irish Times.*

In 1800, about half of a population of 5 million Irish people were Irish speakers. By 1851, only 23 percent of almost 7 million Irish could speak the language, but many of these were bilingual and preferred their children to speak English. From what I can tell, it is very likely that my mother's Irish ancestors spoke Irish when they left Donegal for America.

By the mid-nineteenth century it was obvious English was the language of the future. It was the language in which the state and the courts operated on Irish people. English was the language of education; Irish was banned in the national school system. It was the language in which Irishmen found opportunity and freedom in the British Empire and America.

And so Irish was kicked down from its perch. It was once a high-status language with bards and monks guarding it. Now it was the language of the poor. Even Irish speakers, if they had the most rudimentary English, would sometimes choose never to speak Irish to their children. These parents purposely deprived their children of the intimacy of a common household language in order to give them economic opportunity.

———

Despite all this, by the late nineteenth century, some Anglo-Irish elites, like the descendants of Vikings many centuries before them, found themselves adopting the Irish language as part of their identity. One of these men was Douglas Hyde, a Protestant who saw that previous efforts at Irish national self-assertion were entirely deficient in their appreciation of culture. "Just at the moment when the Celtic race is presumably about to largely recover possession of its own country, it finds itself deprived and stript of its Celtic characteristics, cut off from its past, yet scarcely in touch with its present," he wrote. For Hyde, as for so many others, the Irish language was a romantic endeavor. It was a way of enacting their Irishness that went some ways beyond the grubby transactionalism of liberal societies.

When the Irish compare the language revivals of Hebrew and Irish, they are tempted simply to despair of Irish ability. The similarities are hard to miss. Each language movement talked about itself as an attempt to recover their respective nation's manhood. Each featured people who changed their names as they adopted or matured into nationalist politics. Just as Edward Thomas Kent becomes Éamonn Ceannt, Golda Meyerson becomes Golda Meir. And each of the language revivals was meant to foreshadow and undergird the building of a viable nation-state.

But paradoxically, the fact that Hebrew was a fully dead language gave the Zionists some advantages over the Irish. Hebrew had several competitor languages, all of them weaker or repulsive. A few Zionists believed that they should concede to reality, and that German would be the lingua franca of the Jewish state. Others turned to Yiddish, the language of Jewish ghettos, but which also symbolized exile and hybridity. Being a dead language, Hebrew had no baggage of failure or low social status; it was not considered a language of the poor, or of any Jewish enemy. Jews living in Palestine spoke a number of languages, and they needed a common commercial language.

By contrast, the Irish language was associated with illiteracy and backwardness. And it had one competitor: English, the most important commercial language on earth. Irish had no special role in religion, the way Hebrew did. The Catholic Mass was in Latin. Irish Protestantism was in English.

Being human, the Irish revivalists made their own blunders along the way. There's the story of James Joyce, who took a class on the Irish language and Irish mythology and became disgusted at the teacher's strenuous denunciations of the English language and how he exaggerated the glories of Táin Bó Cúailnge. Joyce retreated to studying Norse mythology instead. The teacher of that Irish class was Patrick Pearse.

But even if the revival failed to make Irish the majority language of Ireland again, Irish is now a language that can be used to write news stories and academic articles and deployed in schoolyard taunts. In the twentieth century, the Irish language grew the ability even to critique its own assigned role as the treasure house of some true, and truly set apart, Gaelic pastoral ideal. Although I'm not yet sure about the accuracy, I laughed my ass off when Alan Titley translated some earthy Irish cursing as "Holy fuckaroni" in his English version of *Cré na Cille*. Maybe some things are best to leave in Irish.

But not all. When my wife and I came to visit your home for the first time, we traveled all around Ireland. And the strangeness of Irish place-names impressed themselves on my wife. Why did so many place-names have these ungainly English syllables: *clon*, *beg*, *bally*, *kil*, and *carrick*? You know they are Irish, do you ever think about them? Suddenly the whole country comes alive. English sometimes collapses them. The *cill* in Kildare is a church, the "church of the oak." But the "*cuill*" in Kilcogy is Irish for forest. *Clon* is a meadow, and so Clonmel becomes a "meadow of honey." Tandragee in Northern Ireland is from the Irish *Tóin re Gaoith*, or "backside of the wind." When you get behind Feltrim in Dublin, you discover the "ridge of the wolves."

Over a century ago, P. W. Joyce wrote, "This great name system, begun thousands of years ago by the first wave of population that reached our island, was continued unceasingly from age to age, till it embraced the minutest features of our country in its intricate network." And yet, many Irish people are unaware of the way the names around them point to landmarks, and beasts, and climate. They've become deaf to the land.

I recently read an Irish commentator saying that every bit of money spent on the Irish language was wasted. Maybe it's sad that languages are in Darwinian competition with one another, he sighs, but some die. Irish-speaking people died too quickly. Their literary rates failed to keep up. We entered into a commercial age, and Irish was not commercial. Irish people are happy to speak

English. In fact, they speak it better than the English. So, let it go.

But the evolutionary game doesn't always end so cleanly. Some creatures decline in one environment but they don't die. They adapt. And I think I caught the barest glimpse of how Irish has adapted itself and can survive lean times in the current environment.

Something like a quarter of a century passed between the time you gave me a hurl and the time I entered a hurling pitch. I experienced another twenty-odd-year gap closing earlier this year. I attended a weekend immersion Irish language course in rural New York, run by Daltaí na Gaeilge. When I arrived, the organizers asked if I had ever been to one of their events before.

Yes, I admitted, when I was four and five years old, with my mother. I showed a few of the older women pictures of my mother and me from that time. And they remembered us. They remembered her. I have occasionally been recognized in the street or in a bar for my disreputable career as a pamphleteer. But this was the first time in my adult life that a stranger recognized me as the son of my mother. And knew my mother because of what language she chose to speak.

I was put in a class made up mostly of children. I was made to re-learn what I had known and forgotten as a toddler. We counted, and practiced saying "Hello" and "How are you?" For me, this is the hardest part of learning a language. The humiliation of being a child again. I make my living with words and I can be astonishingly vain. Learning Irish as an adult means screwing up the simplest things, like counting from *a haon* to *a deich*.

There were only a few people my age at the weekend. There was Antoin, a young teacher who grew up in West Belfast. And Megan from Boston. They knew each other from previous academic conferences on Ulster's culture. But they accepted me, for that weekend at least, as a friend. I know this is sickening for an Irish person like yourself to read, but of course I made fast friends with the man from Belfast. How typical. How obscene. It was Irish Americans who wear their Irishness so lightly—a pin asking for a kiss—romanticizing or even financing men in the Falls Road, who wear their Irishness as a ski mask. Alas, Antoin and I couldn't help it. We both have that thing, of having grown up outside of the Republic, in very different situations, where Irishness must be asserted.

But not too loud. It is customary at Daltaí na Gaeilge to prepare a "party piece," a song, or a poem—preferably in Irish. Antoin, Megan, and I all tried to duck this for drinking and arguing about the Rising.

The night went on, and most of the party retreated for bed. But the drinks flowed on, and something started to happen to the three of us. I believe it was something around each of us that started to crack. Something like the encasing that our common culture imposes on us. I can't speak for everyone, but I can say with some assurance that mass media was my primary teacher growing up. And it taught me and my friends how to conform with one another. It slipped under the table to me a lesson that sincerity is a kind of weakness. That it will be used against me. And that any sentiment at all, anything that could expose you to the danger of ridicule or the genuine possession of an emotion, should be double- and triple-Saran-wrapped in irony. I suppose we do this for safety somehow, as if unwrapped passion itself is so flammable, it would consume our little worlds at the instant we exposed it to open air.

I was getting drunk. And so I grabbed Antoin at one point, and quietly I sang to him a very silly song I know about Ulster, "The Old Orange Flute." He let out big gulps of laughter and an almost maniacal smile. And this new mood descended on the room. Now, for everyone there, I was made to sing the things I sing to my daughter. I tried "The Wind That Shakes the Barley." I don't have a voice for real work on the stage, but for a bar or night like that one, it's pretty good. And then Megan, in a crushingly tender soprano, sang "She Moved Through the Fair." Here it was: We revealed to everyone left, and maybe even to ourselves, that we, yes, the young ones, were romantics too.

Antoin got up and recited the Bobby Sands poem "The Rhythm of Time." By the time in that poem when "the undauntable thought," "screamed aloud by Kerry lakes, / As it was knelt upon the ground," Antoin was sobbing openly and unashamed before us. When was the last time you saw a man in his midtwenties reciting a poem in front of people he just met and croaking out the words through tears?

Yes, all these things were in English. But I believe we were there because something about the Irish language, for us, sets it apart. By the 1960s and '70s, hopes for the complete revival of Irish had been diverted into something more humble, but with radical implications. Preserving Irish took on the character of a voluntary and local resistance to globalization and the reordering of all culture by commerce. Its preservation requires the courage to embrace an identity that could not be bought and sold. I think that is why the experience of coming together to learn this language subtly encouraged us to shed this cumbersome emotional armor, this generational pose of ironic distance from everything, even ourselves.

And to shed it means to recognize the deeper truth about my little foray into this quixotic "useless" language. The die-hard clerical Gaelic Leaguer Rev. O'Hickey complained of the failure to preserve the language: "Are the Irish people going to endure this? If so they deserve the worst that has ever been said of them. They are a people without spirit, without national self-respect, without racial pride, a poor, fibreless, degenerate emasculated, effete race—eminently deserving of the contempt of mankind." I know how the culture around me wants me to respond to a statement like this: with a knowing, dismissive snort. If I'm to respond to it intellectually at all, it is as an academic. "Well, O'Hickey is echoing common tropes about masculinity and nationalism and such and such." If I am to respond the way my education would prompt me, I would say that O'Hickey is being intolerably absolutist.

What the culture insists I am not supposed to do is read those words and feel an honest conviction flooding my heart and stealing my breath. What I am not supposed to do is make vows to wake up your grandchildren each morning with *"Tà an maidan ann. Múclaígí anois, a thaiscí!"*

Many language learners say that they find a new personality in their second language. Already I can see the Irish language gives me access to another part of myself, one that doesn't feel so needful of admiration, that doesn't couch itself in layers of irony and hide behind hand-waving verbal acts of self-creation. I'm determined to learn Irish, because it forces me to be a child and to grow up again. It allows me to become the kind of person who can utter simple convictions and mean them: I bought those Irish language books for my daughter because my mother bought the same books for me. I struggle to learn the Irish language because she struggled to learn it. Because she wanted me to learn it. Because our little routine at night was for her to tell me to "*dún un doras,*" and we would exchange an "*oíche mhaith!*" before I went to bed. Because the history of being Irish is setting yourself an impossible task, then failing to do it over and over again, until one day it is accomplished. My mother tried. I will try again. This isn't mere sentiment. The speech being Irish, the heart must needs be Irish.

It might cost a little money for me to learn a dying language, to graft it onto the tongue of the man of this house. But then the transaction stops being commercial. My children learn it freely, something Irish that is not a product or a brand that fades, but that becomes its own treasure, letting us live off the wealth it generates over a lifetime.

And I can already see the returns coming in. None of your household fits into the category of "competent speakers." You have told me about the image of Irish speakers that you had in childhood, of women that smelled like turf fires, and men that smelled like their fishing nets. You're no good with it, you say. But that is what everyone says. When I have tried my few words of Irish at Dublin Airport, I get the distinct sense that the people working there would rather that an American try to sneak a gun past them than a few words of Irish. They look genuinely pained or even threatened. I know that Irish people can have a genuinely complex relationship with this language that they almost understand. They want it to continue to exist, but they never use even the few words they have.

But when you and your daughters visit, and see these little children's books lying around, you pick up these books and read them to her. All of you dare yourself to do it. My intention was that my daughter learn Irish, but through her, I'm beginning to think all of you have a chance.

Slán,
your son

VII

Reconciliation

O wise men, riddle me this:
what if the dream come true?
What if the dream come true?
and if millions unborn shall dwell
In the house that I shaped in my heart,
the noble house of my thought?

—*Patrick Pearse*

The sun is rising here as I write to you. And a blade of soft orange light is expanding across my dining-room table toward this letter. The kettle is on. Everyone in our kip is still asleep. My little girl is on the couch, her safety guarded by the tangle of blankets and pillows I put on the floor, in case, when I'm not looking, she rolls off. I am happy.

Growing up without a father has meant that I am late to life. Every year, as I enter middle age, some little event that would have happened for just about anyone else in their boyhood finds me. A few years ago it was standing on the hurling pitch with you. Last week, my brother-in-law got me a baseball glove for my birthday. We did a long toss for around half an hour and shot the shit. He had no idea it was my first catch. Another sports milestone a quarter century too late. Life's spectator is finally translated to the field of play.

You predicted that having a child would "send me to the roots." You were right. It's not just the pile of history books and the Irish lessons. My daughter has sent me back to you. And in just the past year I've made my two best memories with you.

Just a few months ago, I visited you on my own. I walked the sites of the Rising during Paddy's week. I walked Northumberland Street. I walked to the General Post Office, and imagined the incredible racket a gunship in the Liffey would make firing on it. I ignored the official tours for my own reading. Another day I got off at Connolly station, then crossed the river and walked to the Abbey Theatre. As an institution, I knew it as the nursery for my heroes.

You knew that we could get standby tickets if we waited for the right time. And there in the theater we watched *The Plough and the Stars*, a play about the lives interrupted, distorted, and lost in the Rising. In the final moments, a dramatic re-creation of "the awesome Wagnerian inferno of smoke and fire" that closed the Rising and destroyed Dublin closed in on you and me.

In the middle of the play, from offstage we hear the voice of Patrick Pearse in hysterical pitch. It was the same quote I heard over and over during this year of commemoration, cited to shame the people who wanted to celebrate his memory and his achievements:

We must accustom ourselves to the thought of arms, to the sight of arms, to the use of arms. We may make mistakes in the begin-

ning and shoot the wrong people; but bloodshed is a cleansing and a sanctifying thing,
and the nation which regards it as the final
horror has lost its manhood. There are many
things more horrible than bloodshed; and
slavery is one of them.

The play is almost perfectly calibrated to play
to your politics and general view, the view of a
man who thinks in terms of labor, that high ideals
of national glory count for nothing against hunger
or illness. In the play all the men are enthralled
by talk of national greatness, while their working-
class wives suffer the destruction it ultimately
wrought.

I have three things to say about it. The first is
that the play uses the old Unionist trick of hiding
the English from view until the second before
Irish violence strikes them. The second is that this
level of romanticism about violence was every-

where during World War I. It was common to nationalist movements all over Europe, and you would find much of it in the Parliament too. You'll find it in Theodore Roosevelt, who lost a child in the war. The third is to understand that Pearse is talking to himself. At this time, he is urging himself to do something quite unusual for someone like him, a melancholic dandy and educationist. Okay, I have a fourth thing to say about it: Pearse is right.

Ireland's modern leaders have come on the radio, interrupting, the happy local commemorations of the Rising, and tut-tut that "sacrifice breeds intransigence." I wonder what it is they can mean. Do they love nothing in life so much as to be intransigent in its defense?

I've been contemplating it on nights like last night, when my little girl started to cry in the middle of the night. I picked her up. I settled her down. And before I fell asleep, I read Patrick Pearse. And in his words, I think I have found the answer. This baby girl in my arms overthrows all uncertainty about it. Manhood is found in sacrifices, offered joyfully. The only liberation worth having is one accomplished in sacrifice.

Sometimes the sacrifices are almost unbearably slight and the rewards returned to them unconscionably large. And that is fine. It is giving me a chance to practice this formula. A slow pitch. Overnight, like most nights, my daughter could not sleep. I gave up my bed and brought her into the dark of the living room. I sang to her quietly, and bounced lightly until she gave up the fight and fell back to sleep. Yes, it is annoying to be up when I need sleep. But subtract the slight feeling of panic about waking up her mother, and what is left is a gentle dance. She falls asleep lying on my chest, and I watch her breathe. She snores contentedly on daddy's chest. Nature asks me for this tiny sacrifice of sleep, through this little imperfection of her youth, and then the joy returned to me I can treasure and hold on to for the rest of my life.

Sometimes, for posterity's sake, the sacrifices demanded are larger. Pearse, above all else a teacher, trained boys for it at St. Enda's, the school he formed to be an example of what Irish education should be. He wanted to use the most progressive educational methods of his day, but in service to fostering the most durable values. He occasionally referred to his methods as discipleship. Pearse considered the school system the English had forced on Ireland—one imposed on them before it was forced on English students— "the most grotesque and horrible of the English inventions for the debasement of Ireland." It was a disaster worse than even the Famine. He indicted it as a "murder machine" that deliberately created human debris. In his mind, the English education system had the same mission Sir Edmund Spenser drew up for Ireland: civilizing the Irish by destroying Irish civilization, absenting the Irish from their national heroes and saints, and robbing them of their language. Borrowing from Eoin Mac-Neill, he compared this system to the separate system set up by Romans and Greeks for educating slaves:

> To the children of the free were taught all noble and goodly things which would tend to make them strong and proud and valiant; from the children of the slaves all such dangerous knowledge was hidden. They were taught not to be strong and proud and valiant, but to be sleek, to be obsequious, to be dexterous: the object was not to make them good men, but to make them good slaves. And so in Ireland.

St. Enda's foreshadowed or invented the idea of education as a tool of decolonialization. It was also a national spectacle. The leaders of Dublin's cultural renaissance and the Gaelic revival would attend the plays put on by St. Enda's boys. People bought pictures of the students. St. Enda's was an innovator in bilingual education. And although Pearse tried to develop a distinctly Irish model of education out of the medieval concept of "fosterage," St. Enda's also very clearly looks like a rival to England's Eton College. Instead of rugby, hurling. In King Arthur's place, Cuchulain. St. George eclipsed by Colmcille. Gaeilge, not English. He wanted freedom for the boys of St. Enda's, freedom from shallow educational methods, freedom to shape a character in the crucible of a school. And this formation of character meant sacrifice. I grant that there is something utterly mad about Patrick Pearse. Imagine receiving this as the headmaster's note in your son's school magazine:

I dreamt I saw a pupil of mine, one of our boys at St. Enda's, standing alone upon a platform above a mighty sea of people, and I understood that he was about to die there for some august cause, Ireland's or another. He looked extraordinarily proud and joyous, lifting his head with a smile almost of amusement. I remember noticing his bare white throat and the hair on his forehead stirred by the wind, just as I had often noticed them on the hurling field. I felt an inexplicable exhilaration as I looked on him, and this exhilaration was heightened rather than diminished by my consciousness that the great silent crowd regarded the boy with pity and wonder rather than with approval—as a fool who was throwing away his life rather than a martyr that was doing his duty. It would have been so easy to die before a hostile crowd: but to die be-

fore that silent, unsympathetic crowd . . .
No one can finely live who hoards life too
jealously: that one must be generous in service, and withal joyous, accounting even
supreme sacrifices slight.

One can dismiss this as insanity or shrink before it. Compared to Pearse's dream, I fear that I
belong to a class of people who have been formed
to be sleek, obsequious, and dexterous. Everything
about the world I work in, the class of people who
are my intended peers, about the education I received in school, and the mass-media formation
given in childhood instructs me to fear more than
anything being the man Pearse would prize as a
"fool." I am taught to be quick, and clever. Not
deliberate or wise. To be marketable, not indigest-
ible. I'm taught to get along, not to be intransigent.

And not just this little social circle, but my
whole life has worked toward this end. All my for-

mation was dedicated to my being free and consciously choosing how to go about my life. I was a fatherless boy. And in my fatherlessness I turned my timidity into slyness. I learned to please people and get from the world what I want, without giving back. In my cynicism I would have rolled my eyes at the idea of becoming hard, proud, and valiant. A matured cynicism would come up with a way of dismissing those words as empty ideology. All this talk of nobility of purpose, a mask for the pursuit of power. This was my way of reassuring myself I never had to be responsible. I never had to be up to it.

Pearse has changed my view of political life. Or, more accurately, reading Pearse with your sleeping granddaughter stretched across me has transformed my views of nearly everything earthly, politics included.

You see, as I entered my adulthood I allowed myself to believe as much as Edmund Burke would give me, that "society is indeed a con-tract . . . not only between those who are living, but between those who are living, those who are dead, and those who are to be born." He expands it to say that "each particular state is but a clause in the great primæval contract of eternal society." But in Pearse's essay "Ghosts" I see the lineaments of the next code, or at least my next code. And a better one than I had before.

Some critics have accused Pearse of masking how modern he was, by talking so much about tradition, and that his true message was discern-ible only by sensitive souls. But in Pearse there is no contradiction between past and future. He was oriented to both at the same time. He acutely felt the intervention of the past on himself. He said that the ghosts of dead men had bequeathed a trust to the living. And he continued, "There is only one way to appease a ghost. You must do the thing it asks you. The ghosts of a nation sometimes ask very big things; and they must be appeased, whatever the cost."

I am not a sensitive soul, but perhaps a kindred one. I have said many sweet things in this letter. But now is the time to be blunt. Pearse feared the death of the Irish nation. I sometimes fear the death of both Ireland and America. He despised the generation previous to his own. And, you know, I have felt that same disgust at yours.

> "*Is mairg do ghní go holc agus bhíos bocht ina dhiaidh,*" says the Irish proverb: "Woe to him that doeth evil and is poor after it." The men who have led Ireland for twenty-five years have done evil, and they are bankrupt. They are bankrupt in policy, bankrupt in credit, bankrupt now even in words. They have nothing to propose to Ireland, no way of wisdom, no counsel of courage. When they speak they speak only untruth

and blasphemy. Their utterances are no longer the utterances of men. They are the mumblings and the gibberings of lost souls. . . .

They have built upon an untruth. They have conceived of nationality as a material thing, whereas it is a spiritual thing. They have made the same mistake that a man would make if he were to forget that he has an immortal soul. They have not recognised in their people the image and likeness of God. Hence, the nation to them is not all holy, a thing inviolate and inviolable, a thing that a man dare not sell or dishonour on pain of eternal perdition.

For Pearse, the last generation are the constitutional nationalists, the Home Rulers who had abandoned the doctrine of full separation from England. They had lost their manhood. There had been four armed rebellions against British rule in the century before Pearse was born, and none in his lifetime. Intentionally or not, Pearse corrects Edmund Burke. For Pearse, a nation is not just a contract but a living thing, found in "the sum of the facts, spiritual and intellectual, which mark off one nation from another." It is something to be intransigent about, as one would be intransigent in the defense of a home.

Going to the roots brought me to consider the Easter Rising. And what it says to me now is that the past reproaches the present on behalf of the future.

I mean this almost superliterally: The ghosts of a nation reproach the living on behalf of posterity. A nation or a society is not merely a contract between the living, the unborn, and the dead; it is a spiritual ecology that exists among them. A nation exists in the things that a father gives to his children, or else he is shamed before his father and grandfather, and his descendants too. The things that are needed for the future.

We have, perhaps fatally, polluted this ecology. We have reversed the process in which humility before the past leads to self-sacrifice in the present and new life and regeneration for the future. We have declared this state of things the end of history, imagining that people can live as consumers only, bored with life.

That loneliness I once felt, a latchkey kid in housing built for broken families. The only child and the man of the house at the same time. That's common now. That feeling of being cut off from the past at a young age. This is becoming a way of life in America. And Ireland is on the way too.

When we do have children we so often have them as consumable objects, as part of our lifestyle choices. We do not receive them as gifts, as living things, inviolate and inviolable. We calculate about them, not worried over what we might give them, but what they take from us. Or, as you know, we simply abandon them. The children we keep, we leave to the care of professionals, who in turn treat them like units of labor to be worked on. We give them over to an education system that euthanizes their imagination, that literally drugs them into obedience. Any individual without a posterity may be a tragedy, or may be a saint. But a nation that is characterized by this fatherlessness, that ignores the real future that is incarnate before us, changes its society in a frightening way.

I believe it causes us to overconsume our natural resources, to overconsume generally, as a form of emotional compensation and distraction from lives wrung out of deeper joys and trials. Instead of leaving our own surplus, we turn the state into a machine for passing on our debts—economic, environmental, social—to a posterity that we do not create. And our posterity, insofar as it exists at all, is left unequipped to meet those debts.

Because we have committed this abuse, naturally we must deafen ourselves to the reproach of the past. We reinvent the murder machine, and turn it on ourselves. The old one worked by making Ireland's past and its heroes invisible to the Irish, thereby depriving them of an identity that could be hostile to Britain. The new murder machine is almost the whole culture now, which works even harder and constantly, not to make the past invisible, but to make it omnipresent and detestable, thereby to deprive us of the conscience of our nation. The murder machine invents little faddish ideologies on which to fail the past, and in doing so it relieves ourselves of its censure.

We are great consumers. We are useless as conservators. Useless in this way, we deepen the pattern, failing to have children, or failing the children we have. We make ourselves sleek, obsequious. Pearse used rhetoric to urge himself on to greater deeds. We use the same to comfort ourselves in backing away from even the most common decency. I've discovered in the letters between you and my mother the legal and moral calculations done over me, what was legal in America, but not yet in Ireland. My mother brought it up to you as a point of discussion, but she quickly dismissed it. She couldn't bring herself to do it. She would make sacrifices, and make a home for me.

Fatherhood teaches me that if we let it, new life comes to restore us. A new life reconciles us as fathers and sons, nations with their history, however turbulent. That is what I've learned in this year and a half since becoming a father.

———

Last year, there was another wedding invitation in my life. This one from Darragh, the cousin I never thought I'd know. When I was a child, he had been a name, but now that you and I are repairing the breach, he is a friend, sometimes a confidant, and a man who will place bets for me. The ones that are not yet legal in America, only in Ireland. He and his household have done well in life, and out of that sense of abundance, he had my whole household come to share in "the big do."

At that wedding, you and I were sharing black beers in the very hotel from which the British shot out the rebels in St. Stephen's Green. My child, your granddaughter, was playing upstairs, perhaps in a room that was used by khaki soldiers as one of the poshest sniper's nests in the history of the empire. A testament that the Irish can accept whatever others dish out. Darragh's wife, I came to learn, was in the touring company for Riverdance. And so we also had testament that night that even Ireland's kitsch can be remade as joy.

And that night you told me your side of one of our stories. You told me about the time you had saved and saved for the plane ticket, only for my mother to disallow you from seeing me after you landed in Newark. She was too upset, she said. And I would be too upset. You went home, having seen your son for only a few minutes.

You told me how, in the following years, your frustration at being unable to see me overcame you. So you researched the times of my recess and lunch at my primary school. And without telling my mother, you flew to America and just presented yourself to me at my school. You made your best friend a coconspirator. He told you he believed you'd both be arrested. You caught so much hell for this from my mother, and from the nuns, and from your own conscience. I had spent years giving you silence, thinking that I was the afterthought in your trip. And here, on this night, I find I was your only thought.

"I felt like a terrorist," you said, recalling it and feeling guilty. The words fell on me like a thunderclap. Our estrangement was real, but in that moment, I learned you had made real sacrifices, taken real risks to see me. You would endure any strife it might cause in your house, and any hatred it occasioned in mine. You could barely lift your eyes up to me as you said that now, having a child of my own, I would understand.

I do.

But I shared with you the other detail of the story, the one that haunted me through all my years of silence. When you had come to the door of my school's cafeteria and my back was to you, that friend of mine said to me, as if it were nothing, "Michael, your dad is here." He had never seen you before. He just looked at you and knew. The simple fact that everyone could see about us—even if, at times, I tried to deny it.

Please, never be ashamed of the things you did to know me and be known by me. No matter how stupid or awful you felt, no matter how strange or upsetting they were to others, even to me. My mother's wish, expressed to you in a letter, was that I should know myself to be Irish. It was an absurd thing to hope for. But maybe a little "terrorism" on your part made it true.

You predicted that my own fatherhood would send me to the roots. Of course it did. Fatherhood makes sense of sacrifice. It is an education that has deepened my ability to be "generous in service, withal joyous." And that is why you and I must, in those small moments we steal now and then in the years we have left, here or in Ireland, make up a little of the time lost between the first time you put the hurl in my hand and the first time I walked onto a hurling pitch twenty-five years later. My daughter must tramp around in the stony gray soil in Monaghan, where you walked to Mass with your grandparents. She should hear you argue for Connolly and class war against me, and me argue for Pearse and the nation against you. We can laugh about our common ancestry with the High

Kings of Ulster, and all that has gotten us in life. You should bring her a little hurl next time you are here. Get her a Dublin jumper. Better yet, Monaghan. What would your grandfather want for her? There is only one way to appease a ghost. You must do the thing it asks you.

You said that our relationship now, as men, is more than you could have rightly hoped. Can't you see that, among all the loves, fears, shames, and uncertainties that belong to us and only us, there is something else that proceeds outward from our relationship? That what we call Ireland is found in the things that pass between us, and reverberate out into the world? To dance up to the line of idolatry, you might say that the life of a nation proceeds from the father and the son.

Because, faced with a child, you do the things you never thought you would do. You dare to do what was unthinkable, or even impossible. You become intransigent and indomitable, proud and valiant, yet willing to be the fool, throwing his life away. You crossed an ocean for the sight of me. I sing a dying language to life. Nations are stubborn things, no?

I never knew your father. And yet, on the night my daughter was born, I called you with the good news. You may still feel like you have no right to me. And that through your absence in my boyhood, you have forfeited any claim upon your granddaughter. I cannot speak to how you feel. But I can tell you that she has a claim on you, her granddad, whatever the accidents, smashups, and misunderstandings that have characterized life between you and me.

Back when you felt like a terrorist, when you were searching in some American school for a son who hardly knew you, could you see that moment?

Ireland is what you gave me, when you wrote letters and sent them into the silence. Ireland is what my mother gave me, when she put those CDs on constant rotation, or hung the *bodhran* proudly in her room. Ireland is what I give to my daughter when I croak out a Fenian tune that would please your father, or when I embarrass myself reading the Irish language books my mother read to me. The men who calculate and search out useful lessons for the present will erect their glass cages and other monstrosities across the landscape. But Ireland will surround her in muddy faerie forts. Her divine knight will come again, "walking from the summer headlands / To His scarecrow cross in the turnip-ground." And through a new, yet always dying, language she will see honey pour out of the meadows. Romantic Ireland is dead and gone; it yet rises from the grave. And underneath a canopy of blush and violet sky, my daughter will see this transfigured Ireland through the songs her daddy sang to her.

These gestures are small rebellions measured against an Empire built on forgetting, in a world that, having given up a sense of duty to posterity, also finds itself a stranger to its past. But the Rising has taught me that when we act, or when we are forced to act on behalf of the future, the past can be given back to us as a gift.

You said that I earned the approval of your father with my songs. If I can do that, you can be my father from now on, in a way that earns the approval of your grandchildren.

> 'Twas Britannia that bade our wild geese go,
> that "small nations might be free";
>
> But their lonely graves are by Suvla's waves or
> the shore of the great North Sea.
>
> Oh, had they died by Pearse's side or fought
> with Cathal Brugha
>
> Their graves we'd keep where the Fenians
> sleep, 'neath the shroud of the foggy dew.

I'm still singing it.

———

I don't know if you can bear to read these words. I am finally ready to answer your question now. Do I have anything to say to you?

I am happy you are my father. I am so happy my daughter has you for her granddad. Tons and tons of love to you and my siblings.

And there is more news. We are expecting another child. Another American-born man who will be taught, against all reason, that he is also Irish. He'll be with us next January. You will come over, and he'll see you at a younger, tenderer age than you first saw me. I can't wait.

Your son,
Michael

ACKNOWLEDGMENTS

During the most challenging period of my life, my wife, Marissa, encouraged the trip to Ireland and to that hurling field in Finglas that formed the first paragraphs of this book and changed the trajectory of all our lives. It was she who sent me "back home" again in 2016. It was she who has made several transatlantic flights while expertly managing our unruly babies. And it was she who welcomed into our lives and our home the wild-rover side of my family, one that had been a mystery to her for almost a decade previously. She made the writing—this life—possible. Marissa, I love you.

I am also indebted to all the men who, at different times in my life, showed me fatherly concern and modeled something of what it was to be a man. First my uncles, Donald and Chris Dougherty, who have never denied me anything I needed, even when it was a kick in the pants. Also my eternal gratitude goes to Lawrence Scanlon, who endured the fatherly burden of listening to me blast my favorite music, and in exchange gave me all the tools one needs to make a livelihood in this line of work. I am also indebted to Tony Saracino, who, at a very crucial time in my adolescence, gave me so many chances to transmute fear into courage. And to the men I call "Father" outside the home too: Fr. James McLucas, Fr. Richard Cipolla, and Fr. Greg Markey.

My gratitude extends to my entire family on all sides, who formed me through argument, clowning around, and ballbusting—love, as I've come to know it. All the Doughertys, Marseks, Torettas, Komosinskis, McCormacks, and Christofalos. And to all the people and places that provided shelter while I was writing, especially my parents-in-law, Ted and Louise. My eternal gratitude to Toni for taking care of our rambunctious children and enduring my ideas at their most half-baked. Also Finbar, Theresa, and all the Sullivan children, who took in my wife and children as I wrote. Thanks to Grace Farms in New Canaan, and their librarian Christina, who provided a home office away from the home office that my kids were screaming in.

I've benefited from the enormous amount of high-quality scholarship that goes into Irish history, and a generation of historians who are slowly overturning the overwhelming prejudices of the age I grew up in: Diarmaid Ferriter, Ronan Fanning, Charles Townshend, R. F. Foster, and Fearghal McGarry. Also, my sincere thanks go to my infinitely patient Irish teacher, Sam Ó Fearraigh, who gave me surprising things to read on Irish culture and from the Irish stage, while teaching me true "sheep-shagger's" Irish.

My survival in adulthood is also owed to the editors who all left an imprint on me, as mentors, confidants, and friends. Chief on that long list is Kara Hopkins who transformed the opinionated kid I was into a better writer than I had any right to be. Scott McConnell and Dan McCarthy also were essential in that same project. Joe Weisenthal, Greg Veis, and Ryan Hockensmith, at various times, gave me encouragement and desperately needed paying gigs. Then there was the set of editors at *The Week* who heard me start babbling about the ideas in this book as early as 2015: Ben Frumin, Ryu Spaeth, and Nico Lauricella. And to Charlie Cooke, who endures so much from me now: my copy, my unimpressive attempts at accents from the

Isles, and my never-ending stream of anti-English insults, sometimes in song.

Then there are all the friends and colleagues who gave me some kind of advice or support in the long run-up to this book: Matt Frost, Yuval Levin, Rich Lowry, Jonathan V. Last, Rod Dreher, Kyle Smith, Ed West, David Frum, Matthew Walther, Helen Andrews, Jay Nordlinger, Jonah Goldberg, Katherine Howell, Alexandra DeSanctis, Jibran Khan, Gabriel Rossman, and Alan Jacobs. Special thanks belong to Matthew Schmitz, who took up the offer to read this project with gusto, and gave it a good shearing at one critical stage. I've been gifted to have peers in this business who are the secret audience I write for, the same people I've been writing for since most of us were young: Reihan Salam, Peter Suderman, Eve Fairbanks, Kevin Williamson, Will Wilkinson, Will Wilson, Joanna Robinson, Julian Sanchez, Ezra Klein, Daniel Larison, Chris Hayes, Rob Montz, Graeme Wood, Conor Friedersdorf, Daniel Foster, and Kerry Howley.

Special thanks go to the sustaining friendship of three men—three fathers—who go before me in all things: Ross Douthat, Freddy Gray, and Pascal-Emmanuel Gobry. I'm also blessed to have friends from my school days who keep me grounded and sufficiently humiliated: Tommy Cairney, Justin Akin, Justin Perez, Peter Tascio, and Jeff Vacca.

And to all the people who made this book happen. My agent, David Larabell, has believed in my work as long as anyone. He and the entire team at CAA have been essential to every part of this book. And to my patient editor and confidante, Bria Sandford, who believed in this project more than any other person on earth besides my wife. Thank you, Bria.

I'd like to thank my Irish siblings, Shelley, Yvonne, and Joe, who have endured their American half brother occasionally invading their childhood home, and the affliction of his late affections. Special thanks also for the hospitality, support, and understanding of Francine, their mother.

And of course to Brendan—my father—whose love has endured all the humiliations, the rejections, the extended silences, and now the absurd spectacle of being my father for almost four decades. He can add this to the list of things we need to make up to each other.